Small Eco Houses
Living Green in Style

Small Eco Houses
Living Green in Style

Cristina Paredes Benítez
Àlex Sánchez Vidiella

Universe

First published in the United States of America in 2010 by
UNIVERSE PUBLISHING
A Division of Rizzoli International Publications, Inc.
300 Park Avenue South
New York, NY 10010
www.rizzoliusa.com

Originally published in Spain in 2010 by
Loft Publications S.L.
Via Laietana 32, 4°, Of. 92
08003 Barcelona
Spain
www.loftpublications.com

© 2010 Loft Publications S.L.

2010 2011 2012 2013 / 10 9 8 7 6 5 4 3 2 1

ISBN: 978-0-7893-2095-7

Library of Congress Control Number: 2010923745

Printed in Spain

Editorial coordinator: Simone K. Schleifer
Assistant to editorial coordinator: Aitana Lleonart
Editors: Cristina Paredes Benítez, Àlex Sánchez Vidiella
Art director: Mireia Casanovas Soley
Design and layout coordinator: Claudia Martínez Alonso
Layout: Cristina Simó Perales
Translator: Cillero de Motta

Front cover: Alberto Plácido, Juan Rodríguez
Back cover: David Wakely

Contents

Introduction

Ecology and sustainability are concepts that currently have great influence on many spheres of life, especially that of architecture. We all agree with the impact of the theories on global warming and thus with the need to reduce our CO_2 emissions and ensure that our lifestyles are more respectful of the environment. As far as architecture that reflects these principles, there have been some significant changes and developments but these efforts remain insufficient. In terms of residential architecture, because of a growing world population, the number of houses needed continues to rise and, as a result, consumption of raw materials has increased and so has the cost to the environment because of transporting these materials. It is, therefore, imperative to search for new building solutions that are environmentally friendly and lead to a reduction in the consumption of materials and energy.

The intention of this book is to bring to our readers' attention the many possibilities offered by sustainable architecture. Being ecologically aware starts with adopting an attitude and assuming certain changes in our daily habits. Recycling garbage, leaving the car at home, and using public transportation or a bicycle are little things that contribute to the sustainability of the planet. But there are other things that we can do in our own homes that can also help to achieve a more sustainable form of architecture, such as using energy-efficient compact fluorescent lightbulbs (CFLs), installing water-flow regulators on all the faucets in the house, and increasing insulation so as to avoid wasting heat in winter.

Ecological architecture deals with various issues throughout the process of building a house and takes account of the ecological footprint a building will leave throughout its entire life cycle, from the moment it is designed to when it is erected and used, all the way until it is pulled down. This volume presents a full selection of options, from houses that have been "disconnected" from the power supply and are self-sufficient to residences that have managed to reduce their heat and electricity consumption thanks to simple methods such as making the most of natural light, cross ventilation, or more efficient thermal insulation. It is hoped that our readers will draw inspiration from these small buildings.

This book aims to bring the concepts of sustainable architecture to a general nonspecialist audience. It is possible that these readers will find concepts such as ecological footprint, environmental impact, recyclable and recycled material, thermal mass, and biomass somewhat daunting. However, in the course of the following pages, these terms and others will be clarified so as to help the reader gain a more precise knowledge of this subject.

The building systems espoused by ecological architecture are divided into two main groups: passive and active. Passive systems are options that use the design of a building to fulfill the thermal needs of a house, eliminating the need for mechanical systems such as air-conditioning, thereby making it more energy efficient. Active systems are those that supply energy to residences, using renewable sources such as solar power.

Water savings

Ecomaterials

Active systems

Passive systems

Prefabs

Water Savings

Water is an essential resource that is in short supply and should not be squandered. Because of global warming and its accompanying drought and desertification, it is becoming increasingly urgent to manage water rationally and adopt a new culture of water use.

There are various ways to save water in the home. One of the first things to do is to check that there are no leaks in the pipes. Other simple actions that save water are to take showers instead of baths, install water-flow regulators on all the faucets, install toilets with a water-retention device or a water-saver flush kit, and buy more energy-efficient electrical appliances. Install sprinklers and timers in gardens and backyards. Plant indigenous vegetation that thrives on the amount of rainfall in the area, rather than plants that require extensive watering. Another system that is widely used to improve water management is the treatment of gray water and rainwater.

Gray water refers to the water generated by a household, i.e., the water from showers and baths, and from washing machines and dishwashers. This type of water is useful for watering gardens. It differs from sewage, or black water, because it does not contain the bacteria *E. coli*. Black water can be treated for reuse in toilets. Avoiding the unnecessary use of drinking water conserves a significant amount of this resource, not to mention it saves on water bills, as well. Untreated gray water cannot be used to flush the toilet, since it might lead to bad smells and stains if left for more than a day.

Rainwater is harvested from rainfall and is used for other purposes, including watering gardens and cleaning both inside and out. Rainwater is also used for dishwashers and washing machines. A good circuit for collecting rainwater can be achieved by installing a pipeline that runs from the roof down to a home's water tank. The capacity of the tank should be determined by the amount of rainfall in the area in which the property is located and the needs of the household. This will guarantee an ample water supply for the uses required. There are systems that use rainwater stored in the tanks but also connect to the conventional water supply as and when necessary, thus ensuring that there is always water available. It is also possible to reuse the water from swimming pools when they are refilled. This follows the same principle as the rainwater system: the water that is recovered can be used for watering the garden and outdoor cleaning.

Ecomaterials

One of the main premises of sustainable architecture is the return to the very origins of architecture. An aspect most associated with this philosophy is the choice and use of building materials. The use of local raw materials is always less costly, not only in terms of the economic value of the material— if it is from a local source, it is likely to be more abundant in that area and therefore cheaper—but also because of the reduced environmental costs of shipping it, as the fuel consumption and CO_2 emissions generated in the transportation of such material will be lower.

Another aspect is the use or adaptation of building techniques and materials that have been around since ancient times, such as adobe. Using age-old techniques might be a sustainable option for building a home, as long as its stability and safety are guaranteed.

The use of so-called natural materials should also be taken into consideration. Grouped together under this umbrella term are materials that require very little in the way of manufacturing processes. Each artificial process, from the extraction of the material or its initial manufacturing process to the time when it rolls out of the factory, has a cost both in terms of energy and impact on the environment. This means that using materials that require minimal processing will be more sustainable. With a variety of natural materials on hand, and, especially in places where these materials are abundant, it has become easier for end users to demand and incorporate materials that are environmentally friendly. The most widely known of these are stone, wood, and bamboo. There are also a number of treatments of these materials, such as the absence of varnish or the use of lacquers, that are respectful of the environment. Straw, which is used for insulation purposes, is another natural material that can be used in construction. Other environmentally friendly insulators are bricks made from compressed vegetable fibers, sand-concrete mixtures, and recycled materials; while all of these go through a manufacturing process, the use of recycled material, renewable resources, or less water than is needed to make standard bricks is a significant development in sustainable housing.

In the category of green building materials are certified materials. One of the most significant is certified wood, or timber that comes from well-managed forests and plantations. This type of wood has not been taken from unprotected forest areas, which guarantees the sustainable management of this raw material and helps guard against the disappearance of the planet's green areas. Two of the most important associations ensuring the controlled origin of the wood are the Forest Stewardship Council (FSC) and Pan-European Forest Certification Council (PEFCC).

There are some techniques that use natural materials such as rammed earth, which is a mixture of local soil and a small amount of cement. This mixture is poured onto the formwork and pressed. The result is a stable, safe construction using earth from a local source.

There are several other types of components and materials that can be used in sustainable architecture. Recyclable and recycled materials are common, the former being materials that can be easily reused and the latter being compounds made from waste or other components. It is important that they not generate any waste either during manufacture or once their useful life is over.

Materials that have been reclaimed, such as wood and many of the natural materials described above, are materials that can be given a second life. For instance, the timber from construction can be used to form part of the beams in a new house; stones from the excavation can be used to build another property nearby, and so on. The reuse of such items means that because local materials are used, savings are made in transportation, and, therefore, in CO_2 emissions. It is also possible to retrieve other waste materials from industrial or urban sources to form part of some of the elements in a house, including railings and banisters, window frames, and cladding.

Active Systems

Conventional energies are those derived from fossil fuels and nuclear energy. Active systems harness and use the power generated from renewable or alternative sources of energy: power from inexhaustible natural resources. The best-known sources of such power are solar, wind, and thermal, although biomass, hydraulic, and geothermal energy have gained in popularity. Because today's society is more environmentally aware, there is now a greater demand for such technology.

One of the most widely known renewable energies is solar power. Sunlight provides the planet with considerably more energy than is consumed. Sunlight is used by solar panels to generate heat or electricity, thus avoiding the need to consume conventional energy. There are two types of panel: thermal solar panels, which capture the sun's rays and transform them into thermal power, and photovoltaic panels, which transform the sunlight into electricity.

The use of thermal solar panels reduces or eliminates the consumption of gas and diesel fuel, along with any other type of conventional energy used for heating and hot water. In most cases, installing a solar conversion valve on an existing system is possible. Using thermal panels reduces both CO_2 emissions and the number of hours a boiler would be working. Hence, fuel consumption is also lower.

Photovoltaic solar panels convert solar radiation into an electric current, which can then be harnessed to power any appliance. Manufacturing this type of panel requires more complex technology than is used for manufacturing solar thermal panels; therefore, the latter is much more widely available. There are various different types of photovoltaic panels from which to choose, depending on the needs of the dwelling and the characteristics of the local climate. When calculating the number of panels that will need to be installed, attention should be paid to the amount of power required in the home. Even if the number of panels needed exceeds the amount of space available to house them, the use of fewer panels will still reduce conventional electricity consumption.

A residential system for generating electricity using photovoltaic panels can be based on three possible solutions: as an autonomous circuit for small installations; as a support system for the electricity used in the home; or as a production system connected to the mains.

Properties that only use clean electric power are known as "off-grid" homes. These homes are completely disconnected from the conventional electricity grid and receive their power supply by harnessing active or passive strategies.

Another term often mentioned when speaking about active systems is *biomass*. Biomass is the organic material generated through a forced or spontaneous biological process, which is used as a source of energy.

A common error is the use of the term biomass as a synonym for the useful energy it can generate. Useful energy can come from the direct combustion of biomass (wood, nutshells, etc.) or from fuels derived from it through physical or chemical change (such as the methane gas generated by organic waste), although there is always some loss in the case of the latter.

The energy harvested from biomass that is best for residential architecture comes from the direct combustion of natural biomass in stoves that burn wood or pellets, or that use fuel for heating that comes from energy crops, although this can also generate CO_2 emissions.

Another active system seen in residential architecture is geothermal energy, which is obtained by harnessing the heat from underground. This technology can be installed in any type of newly constructed building, or even in buildings that are already standing. This type of energy can be used to heat the home and provide hot running water, and also helps to keep the house cool by transferring the heat underground. The geothermal HVAC system transfers or extracts heat from the earth through a set of collectors buried in the ground with a water and glycol solution circulating through them. This system eliminates dependence on external energy, generates minimum waste, and has a low environmental impact. It enhances the appearance of the building since there are no external elements on the walls or roof; it is also silent and can be used in conjunction with other renewable energies.

Another active system available is the one consisting of micro wind turbines. These turbines are similar to larger versions of wind energy generators, but their energy is produced for private consumption. Their application is very useful, particularly in places that an electricity supply cannot reach or is nonexistent, such as rural areas with schools, medical centers, or remote tourist facilities. When installed directly on the site where the energy is to be used, they can provide up to 30 percent of the energy consumed by each household, and they have less visual impact, lower costs, improved efficiency, and a greater level of sustainability. The use of these turbines is subject to regulations and technical specifications governing aspects of their use, such as the maximum distance at which these facilities should be located from the place of consumption and the power required and permitted for each property.

Passive Systems

Buildings that are erected using passive systems (also known as bioclimatic buildings) heat the home using nonmechanical methods, thereby optimizing natural resources.

When designing a building, it is important to take into account where the sun rises, the local climate, and the needs of the occupants. Daylight should be used to the fullest, which will both reduce the use of electricity for lighting and, by harnessing the warmth from the sun, lower heating costs. The concept of thermal mass defines the capacity of a building material, such as concrete, to store heat from the sun's rays and release it back into the atmosphere hours later. Thus, if we let the sun enter a living room with concrete walls or flooring, the walls or flooring will radiate heat at night, making it unnecessary for heat to be generated.

The climate in each region will influence the building's orientation and the inclusion of certain energy-saving components, which in combination, will offer the house the best possible heating and cooling conditions year-round. In hot climates, for example, the design of the house should be analyzed to guard against overexposure to the sun, with the house being fitted with cooling systems to keep the temperature down. The eaves and slope of the roof could be designed in consideration of the changes in the angle of incidence of sunlight during the day and the seasons and thus, for example, protect the house from receiving too much sun during the warmer months.

A green roof—a roof that is partially or completely covered with plants—is another alternative for regulating the temperature of a house. Compared to a traditional roof, it is a much better insulation system. The benefits include the management of rainwater and reduced energy costs. In addition, green roofs or covers also reduce the "heat island" effect found in large cities. The breathability of such roofs and the shade provided by plants cools a building. This reduction in temperature means that there is less need for air-conditioning. This system extends the life of the roof and achieves a better standard of soundproofing, which is a must in noisy areas such as cities or near airports and industrial sites. Likewise, the use of plants such as creepers on the walls of the property contributes to energy savings.

Another solution that promotes energy savings is the Trombe wall. This system entails painting a wall a dark color and installing a pane of glass in front of it so as to create an air chamber. Vents in the wall enable the warm air, which is less dense, to rise and penetrate the building. An opening lower in the wall enables the cooler air to exit. As these vents can be opened or closed as needed, the house can be ventilated or cooled, for example, by allowing the exit of warm air in the summer.

The ventilated facade is a system for insulating walls that consists of several layers of a material with space between the layers. These exterior enclosures are composed of a number of sheets, with the outside finish or siding being a composite of various materials such as natural stone, or metal or plastic paneling. These top layers are fitted in place, leaving a slight gap to ventilate the chamber through the joins that have been created. This provides thermal insulation that is attached to the inner wall, which is also permanently ventilated, thus preventing any condensation. With this type of facade, there are fewer thermal bridges—areas where materials that are poor insulators come into contact, thereby increasing temperature loss or gain. In fact, these thermal bridges virtually disappear.

Installing double-paned windows also offers substantial improvements in both thermal and acoustic insulation. If the window frames are made of a material that is a poor heat conductor, thereby creating a thermal break rather than a thermal bridge, the insulation will be even more effective.

The presence of water, whether from a fountain or a small pond, will affect the temperature of its surroundings, due to the fact that as the water evaporates, it cools the air. Also, if the house has a shady inner courtyard, it is a good idea to grow some plants there. If the residence has land around it, the trees and vegetation will provide shade and shelter from the wind, as well as offer more privacy.

Another of the more popular strategies used in conjunction with sustainable architecture is cross ventilation. If the layout of the house has taken account of the air currents in the area, and the locations of the windows, doors, and balconies have been designed successfully, such currents can be used to cool the property. It might even mean that the house does not require any form of air-conditioning. Thanks to the effectiveness of cross ventilation, even where the design is not perfect, the air currents may be enough to reduce the need for air-conditioning.

The installation of awnings, shutters, and eaves will help regulate the temperature of the property. The shutters provide protection from the heat and create a second layer of insulation, which is useful in both summer and winter. Eaves provide fixed shade and the awnings can be lowered or taken up as needed. Blinds have the same function.

Prefabs

Another trend in green architecture is based on prefabricated buildings. Mass production drives the cost down and such buildings are easier and faster to erect. These systems also lead to savings in CO_2 emissions, since excessive transportation of materials is avoided, and the environmental impact on the natural surroundings is lower, particularly in houses located in the country or mountain regions. The progress made in researching building materials and techniques has also enhanced the durability of such properties. The use of certain prefabricated elements or materials, even in conventional architecture, will contribute to developing buildings that are faster and cheaper to build, and more environmentally friendly.

Watershed

FLOAT Architectural Research and Design

Wren, Oregon

6.5 m² / 70 sq. ft.

© Gary Tarleton

13

Small ECO Houses

The owner of this house is a writer, whose main wish was to have a small studio in which to be able to write in peace, watch the birds, and listen to the sound of the rain. The property is located in the Willamette Valley, alongside the Marys River. The architects looked at ways to build the shed with the least possible impact on the environment—so with no road access, and no electricity use or excavation work. The component parts of the building were manufactured at the factory and then assembled in situ.

There is a concrete base to support its weight and allow the rainwater to drain along the steel structure forming the frame of the shed. It also has wood cladding mounted on the frame with stainless-steel bolts, and the double-paned windows have been slotted into dado channels. Since the structure does not have any joints, either in the steel frame or wooden cladding, the studio can be changed, moved, or recycled—even piece by piece if necessary.

In keeping with the requirements of the client, polycarbonate was used to build the roof and produce a soft light inside, and also to enhance the sound of the rain.

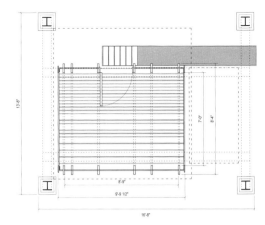

Floor plan

Prefabricated construction, reducing CO_2 emissions from transportation and minimizing impact on the environment; double-paned windows

Many windows to provide natural light and cross ventilation; double-paned glass for insulation; polycarbonate roof to diffuse light; overhang for shade

Minimal environmental impact, due to planned low-tech approach with no road access, and no electricity use or excavation work

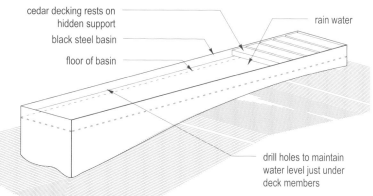

cedar decking rests on
hidden support

rain water

black steel basin

floor of basin

drill holes to maintain
water level just under
deck members

Entrance and reflecting pool

The property has been
constructed by mounting the
prefabricated parts, which
are easy to put together and
take apart again. The design
consists of a steel framework, a
polycarbonate roof, and a wooden
structure on concrete pads.

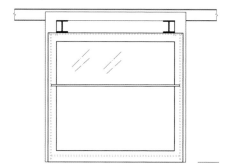

North elevation

There is a generous overhang above the wooden structure of the studio, which provides shade during the day and uninterrupted views of the meadow.

The building has many windows affording panoramic views of the landscape and observation of birds, which act as a source of inspiration for the writer. The interior is simple, with the desk occupying the main area.

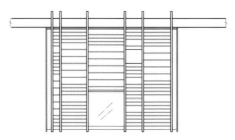

West elevation

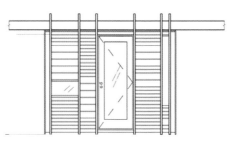

East elevation

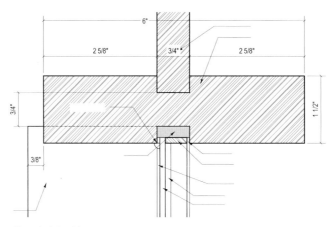

Plan and window joinery

Joshua Tree

Hangar Design Group

Mobile

36 m² / 387.5 sq. ft.

© Hangar Design Group

This prefab home was first presented to the public at the Milan Fair held in 2008 and was a great success with fairgoers, who formed long lines to take a look inside. The architects designed the property as a mountain retreat or vacation home, drawing their inspiration from mountain retreats in the Alps, with their gabled roofs. The building materials include coated steel, zinc, titanium, and wood, which together form a compact structure. For the cladding on the outer walls, large sheets of steel, zinc, and titanium were used; they were placed in position using the method traditionally used with wooden shingles. The interior, which receives a generous amount of natural light, is divided into two bedrooms, a kitchen, and two bathrooms. The interior layout is such that these two spaces can be reorganized in keeping with the tastes and needs of each user.

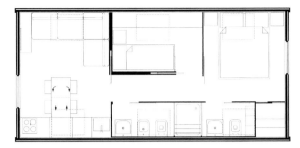

Floor plan

Elevation

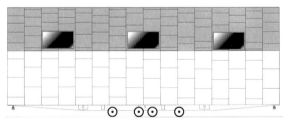

Elevation

Recyclable and reusable materials, such as sheets of titanium and zinc, and panels made of larch wood and steel

Skylights to provide natural light and cross ventilation; wood to keep the inside of the house warm

Constructed off-site to reduce CO_2 emissions from transportation and minimize the impact on the environment

The design of this prefab makes it
easy to transport and adapt to the
different types of terrain on which
it might be located. Furthermore,
it also has a low price.

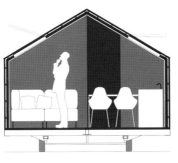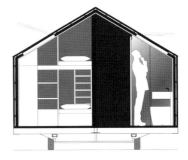

Sections

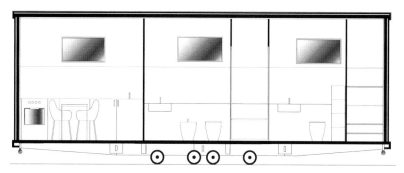

Section

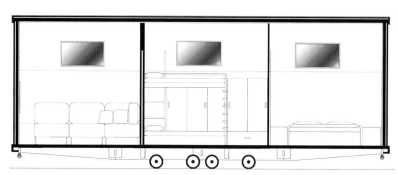

Section

The architects have paid special attention to the use of sustainable resources. The use of timber keeps the inside of the building warm or cool, without any need for heating and air-conditioning systems.

There are several openings
in the roof, which enable
natural light to enter. These
skylights can be opened to
provide natural ventilation.

The plumbing, lighting, and waste-removal systems have been designed in such a way that no trace is left behind when the cabin is moved to another location.

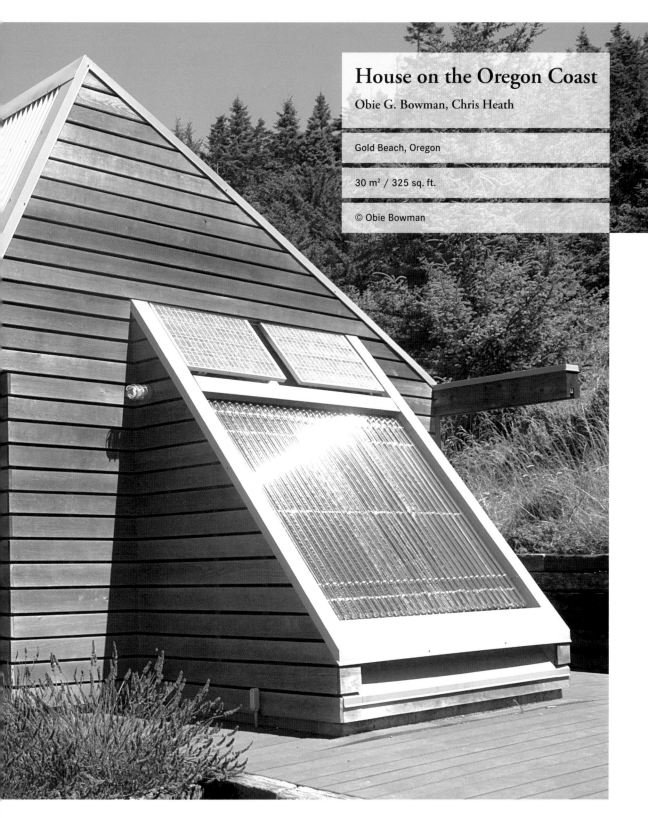

House on the Oregon Coast

Obie G. Bowman, Chris Heath

Gold Beach, Oregon

30 m² / 325 sq. ft.

© Obie Bowman

T his small, environmentally friendly, and off-grid cabin with views over the Pacific Ocean was designed as a guesthouse and studio. It is energy self-sufficient and its frame responds to geological instability, harsh climate conditions, and exposure to the sun. The house is built on a foundation designed to withstand earth movements and is steadied by four pairs of beams that can withstand winds up to 90 miles per hour (145 km/h). Solar panels on the house and others some distance away provide the electricity the house requires. Water for domestic use comes from a shallow well and from collected rainwater and is stored in tanks located up the slope. The cladding materials were chosen for their strength and ease of maintenance. The featured material is locally grown Port Orford cedar, the planks arranged in horizontal rows to allow for seasonal shrinkage and expansion. The composite roof is essentially inert.

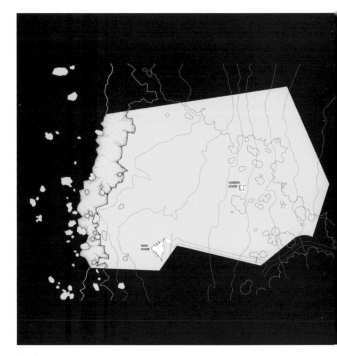

Site plan

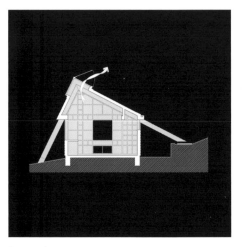

Cross section

 Rainwater collection; water tanks

 Recycled, locally sourced, and certified materials, such as cedar; low-maintenance materials

 Integrated and remote photovoltaic panels

The local vegetation has been
respected, with the exception
of some lavender planted
next to the rear facade.

The frame of this small studio
is stable and can withstand the
strong winds blowing in the area.
The materials used are adapted
to the climate conditions and
require little maintenance.

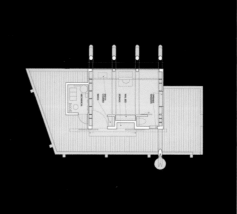

Timber beams funnel the rainwater
into tanks. A membrane filters
solid particles and prevents
them from entering the tank.

Floor plan

The thermal mass of the dark
concrete floor slab stores heat,
which warms the small space.

Casa XS

BAK Arquitectos

Mar Azul, Argentina

52 m² / 559 sq. ft.

© BAK Arquitectos

Mar Azul is a seaside resort located some 250 miles (402 km) from Buenos Aires. The predominant vegetation of this terrain is pine forest, a factor that strongly influenced the project. The brief called for minimal environmental impact on the site, the use of low-maintenance materials, and rapid construction. The solution was a long and low concrete prism. Concrete is low maintenance, impermeable, and resistant. It is also highly flexible and fast to build with. The surrounding vegetation provides shelter and shade during the summer months, but it also prevents light from reaching the house in the fall. To remedy this drawback, the house's openings were specifically positioned to maximize daylight, particularly at both ends of the prism. Durable and low-maintenance quebracho wood was used to make the front door and to clad some exterior areas.

 Durable, low-maintenance or maintenance-free materials

 Well-positioned windows to provide natural light; concrete slab roof to keep the house cool during the summer months; trees for shade in the summer

 Minimal environmental impact; preservation of vegetation cover

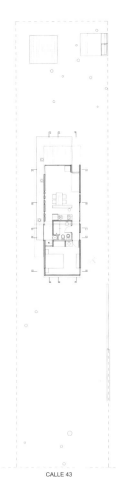

CALLE 43

Site plan

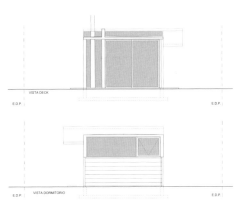

VISTA DECK

E.D.P.   E.D.P.

E.D.P.   VISTA DORMITORIO   E.D.P.

Elevations

The concrete slab roof provides the necessary protection from heat during the months the house is used. The compact concrete is also impermeable.

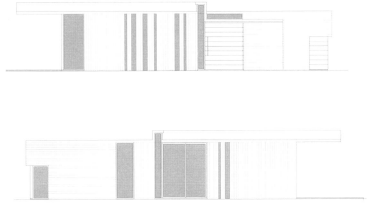

Elevations

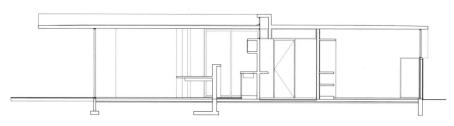

Longitudinal section

Cross sections

No landscaping was done
so as to avoid affecting the
native vegetation; no grounds
maintenance is required other
than removing dead trees.

The windows and openings on the prism were specially positioned to make up for the lack of natural light without compromising privacy. There is a large window in the bedroom wall and windows in the upper part of the bathroom wall.

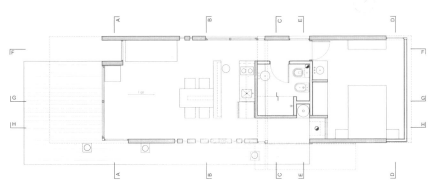

Floor plan

Rincon

Marmol Radziner Prefab

Mobile

61 m² / 660 sq. ft.

© Tyler Boye

One of the latest designs from the Marmol Radziner Prefab venture, founded in 2005, is the Rincon prefabricated module. This and the firm's other models are factory built and delivered completed to the site. Prefabricated construction is beneficial for the environment as it lowers building materials expenses and transportation costs, and factory production reduces the environmental impact on the final site. CO_2 emissions are also lower, as materials do not need to be transported, only the house, once it has been assembled. The Rincon module is the largest of their series of single-module accessory buildings. It features one bedroom, a full kitchen, a bathroom, a living area, bamboo flooring, and a large outdoor deck. The main materials are steel and glass. Homeowners can choose from a number of custom sustainable features. Solar panels, for example, allow the house to function off-grid, generating from 100 watts to 2 kilowatts. Custom additions of insulation with recycled materials, recycled steel, LED lighting, nontoxic paints, and glass with superior insulation and UV protection are also possible.

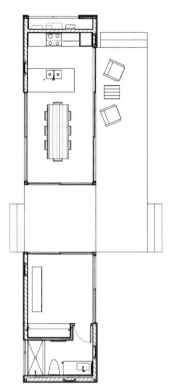

Floor plan

Recycled and recyclable materials such as steel and bamboo; glass with 39 percent higher insulation than standard; FSC-certified wood; nontoxic paints; insulated glass with UV protection

Photovoltaic panels; energy-efficient appliances; LED lighting; on-demand hot water heater

Insulated panels; glass expanses favoring cross ventilation; shaded porches, reducing the need for air-conditioning

The sliding walls blur the limits between interior and exterior and can also be used to create cross ventilation. The porches provide shade in summer, reducing the need for air-conditioning.

The hot water tank works
on demand, saving at least
20 percent of the energy used
by conventional water heaters.

Structural insulated panels reduce
the need for electricity for heating
and cooling by 12 to 14 percent.

Gable Home

University of Illinois

Urbana-Champaign, Illinois

75 m² / 807 sq. ft.

© University of Illinois

T his home was designed to be built in the flat landscape of the American Midwest. The house borrows from the endangered vernacular architecture of farmhouses and barns, iconic features of the midwestern landscape.

For this project, reclaimed barn siding was cleaned and repainted for reuse. Wood from a demolished grain silo was cleaned and treated with linseed oil before being used to build the exterior decking. Despite the dimensions of the house, the interior is spacious and comfortable. The interior walls hang from a structural frame made of bamboo, with a high ceiling that enhances the feeling of spaciousness. The insulation scheme was designed with the aim of obtaining the rigorous Passive House certification. Photovoltaic panels on the southern roof produce more electricity than is required to operate the appliances in the house.

The house was designed to be transported to its final site. It is currently in Illinois, where a long-term study of its energy performance is being carried out.

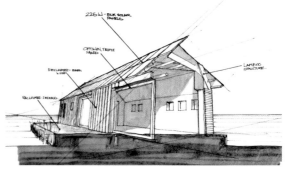

Sketch

Exploded perspective view

Prefabricated construction; recycled and recyclable materials, such as bamboo

Photovoltaic panels

House orientation to make maximum use of heat and light from the sun; thick insulation; large windows to provide light and cross ventilation

3-D renderings

Renderings in 3-D show the simplicity of the house design. The timber boards and the shape of the roof are the most outstanding features, recalling the architecture of farmhouses and barns in the region.

Structure perspective

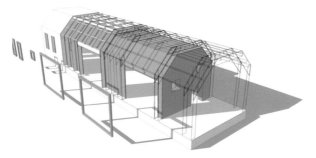

Perspective of the structure interior

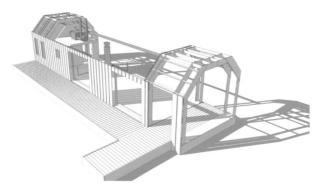

Perspective of reused timber boards

The south facade makes use of the sun with both passive and active strategies. Expansive windows let natural light and heat into the house. The solar-panel array on this roof turns solar energy into electricity.

The reuse of building materials
from demolished structures—an
old silo in this case—is yet another
way of achieving sustainable
architecture. Savings are made
on materials, manufacturing, and
transport.

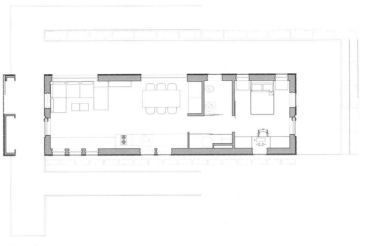

Floor plan

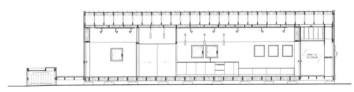

Longitudinal section

Cross section

The floor plan and sections
show the size of the spaces.
The distribution can be adapted
to provide more bedrooms or
additional spaces.

Wood Cabin on Lake Flathead

Andersson Wise Architects

Polson, Montana

77 m² / 830 sq. ft.

© Art Gray

T his small wood cabin is located near a granite and slate outcrop and has views over Lake Flathead, in the perfect spot to enjoy the pine forests of this part of Montana and the ospreys that nest in this natural setting in the northern United States. The purpose of the building was to create a home that shared this natural space and that showed almost reverential respect for its flora and fauna. This house can be considered 100 percent passive: it is completely off-grid and there has been minimal impact on the site—both before and after construction. The cabin rests on six steel pillars, delicately anchored by solid concrete foundations. This means that neither the slope nor the features of the terrain were modified. The interior is open plan; there is only one bedroom, a living area, and a small kitchen and bathroom. The interior's wood floor continues outside onto a cantilevered deck and a bridge that spans the slope.

Site plan

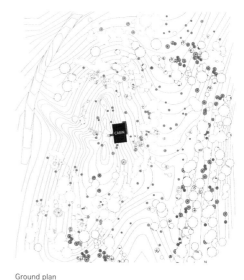

Ground plan

Recyclable materials; construction off-site

Off-grid house; large windows to provide natural light

Minimal environmental impact due to structural pillars and foundations being laid by hand, not machines; preservation of local vegetation

The foundations were laid by
hand; no machinery was used.
The timber boards were sawn
off-site and assembly was done
in a way that did not disturb
the birds nesting nearby.

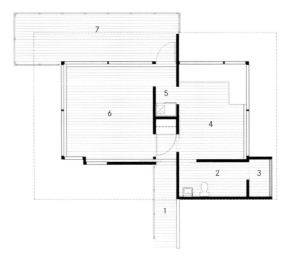

1. Bridge
2. Bathroom
3. Outdoor shower
4. Bedroom
5. Kitchen
6. Living area
7. Deck

Floor plan

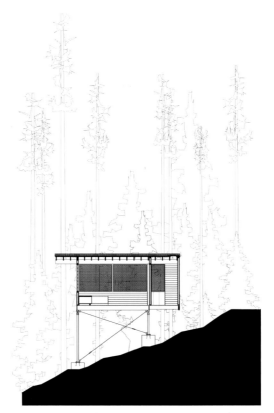

This structure on pillars managed not to alter the site. A bridge leads to the single floor. This was the best option for this brief, which was to coexist with nature.

Section

The glass walls of the living area let
in light, reducing the dependence
on electricity. They also allow the
imposing scenery to be enjoyed.

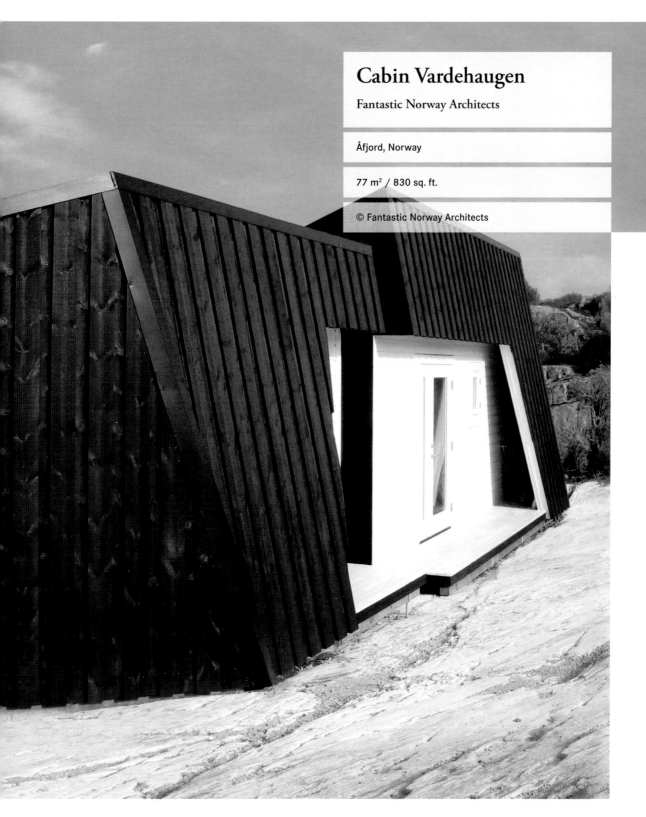

Cabin Vardehaugen

Fantastic Norway Architects

Åfjord, Norway

77 m² / 830 sq. ft.

© Fantastic Norway Architects

This house is located on the Fosen peninsula at 115 feet (35 m) above sea level. Rocks, sea, and mountains dominate this abrupt landscape. This small house is laid out in the style of traditional Norwegian village homes, typified by the provision of sheltered exterior spaces.

A detailed study of the wind and its intensity in the area, made with the help of local residents and Anne Brit Børve's doctoral thesis on building design for cold climates, was vital for the project to be built. The orientation of the structure is a foil for the wind, deflecting it from the core of the house to prevent energy loss. Protected from the wind, external areas of the house are transformed into living areas, a design element that allows the surface area of the structure to be reduced. The black roof helps to heat the interior, just as the double-paned windows allow more natural light to enter. A water filter system is one of a list of sustainable elements featured in this house.

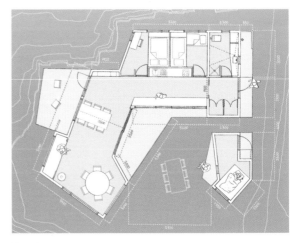

Floor plan

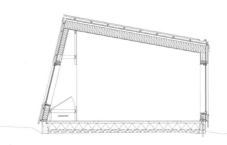

Sections

 Water filter system

 Biomass stove

 House orientation to prevent excessive exposure to wind and energy loss; black roof to absorb heat from the sun; large windows to provide natural light; double-paned windows

 Orientation that prevents the excessive exposure to the wind and the loss of energy

The orientation of the house has resulted in exterior spaces that are protected from the strong winds so that the rocky landscape and sea can be enjoyed. These spaces offer a more direct contact with nature.

The shape of the house was
specifically designed to provide
protection from the strong winds.
The guest wing also serves as
a foil to the prevailing winds.

Heat and energy come from
natural biomass—a wood-
burning stove in this case—which
is more environmentally
friendly than burning fossil
fuels for heating would be.

The large communal area
features floor-to-ceiling windows
that let light inside and reduce
electricity use, particularly in
the summer months when there
are more hours of daylight.

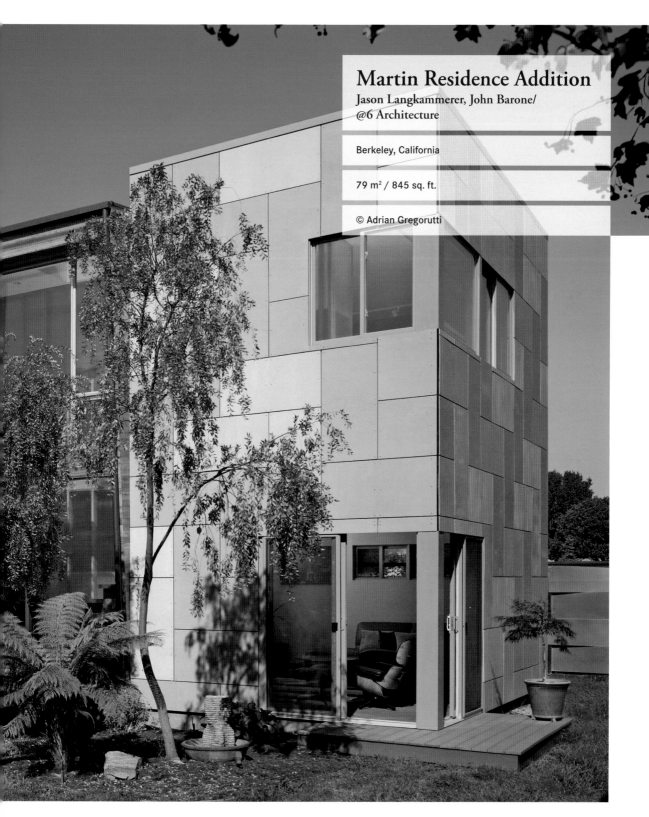

Martin Residence Addition

Jason Langkammerer, John Barone/
@6 Architecture

Berkeley, California

79 m² / 845 sq. ft.

© Adrian Gregorutti

The Martin residence was extended by adding a small two-story volume: a living area with one bathroom and one bedroom. This modern structure is adjacent to the original 1940s house. The contemporary design of this addition arose with a clear purpose: to consume fewer resources. Advanced assembly techniques were incorporated during the design process to reduce the amount of material needed, which also meant cost savings. The structure is clad in a series of prefabricated, impermeable fiber-cement panels that protect it from the rain. This cladding allows the facade to be ventilated, which prevents the formation of mold and pest infestation.

The interior features a polycarbonate wall on one side of the staircase so that natural light is diffused throughout the interior. The double-height glass wall on the south facade generates passive heat in cold months and, with the skylight on the roof, acts as a solar chimney. The south-facing roof offers a perfect location for photovoltaic panels.

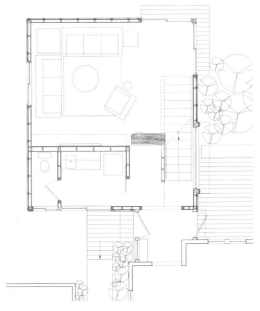

Upper level

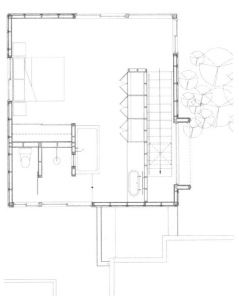

Lower level

Recyclable materials such as bamboo panels; recycled materials such as timber stairs

House orientation to make maximum use of heat and light from the sun and to provide cross ventilation; large glass wall to provide natural heat and, with the skylight, act as a solar chimney

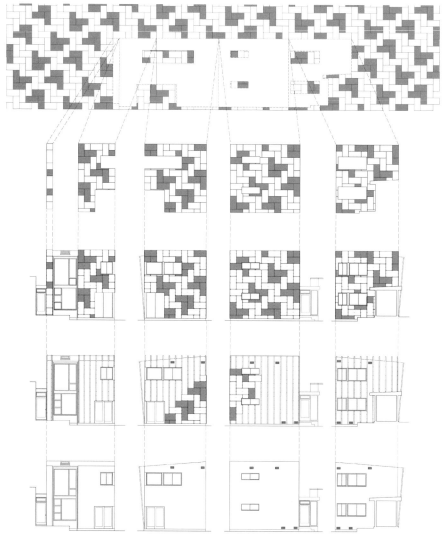

Diagram of fiber-cement cladding

The fiber-cement panels
were cut in a factory to exact
measurements in order to prevent
waste. They are in two colors
and were placed over wood
slats in a herringbone pattern.

Lower level of the main residence and the addition

Cabinets, bathroom furnishings, and flooring feature recyclable bamboo panels. The stairs connecting the two levels are made from recycled timber.

Huis JP

Change Architects

Bilthoven, The Netherlands

86.7 m² / 933 sq. ft.

© Pieter Kers/Change Architects

This 1930s house required an extension to satisfy the needs of its occupant family. Its subsequent remodeling took into account several criteria for improving the comfort and sustainability of the house. The sustainability principles applied by the architects went further than just utilizing passive systems: they sought a flexible architecture that could adapt to all of its owners' needs not only in the present but also in the future, to avoid having to undertake more renovations. The addition was built to enhance the entry of natural light in order to reduce the use of electricity during the day. Glass doors open to the exterior, creating ventilation during the summer months and blurring the boundaries of the garden. New, well-insulated facades replaced the old ones. The facades are clad in FSC-certified wood.

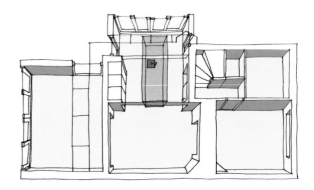

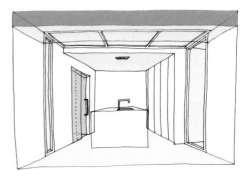

Renderings

 FSC-certified wood

 Orientation to make maximum use of heat and light from the sun and to provide cross ventilation; glass doors and windows to provide natural light and cross ventilation; insulation

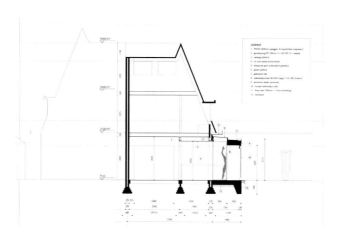

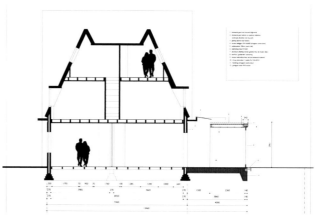

Sections

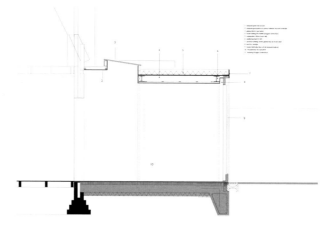

Addition construction detail

The new rooms increase the
floor space while improving the
insulation of the rest of the house.

The dark wood on the facade
is FSC-certified. The use of this
regulated material helps to prevent
deforestation on the planet.

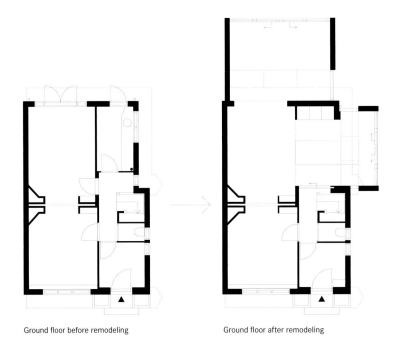

Ground floor before remodeling

Ground floor after remodeling

The addition features extensive use
of glass, which enables the interior
of the communal areas to receive
daylight, reducing electricity use.

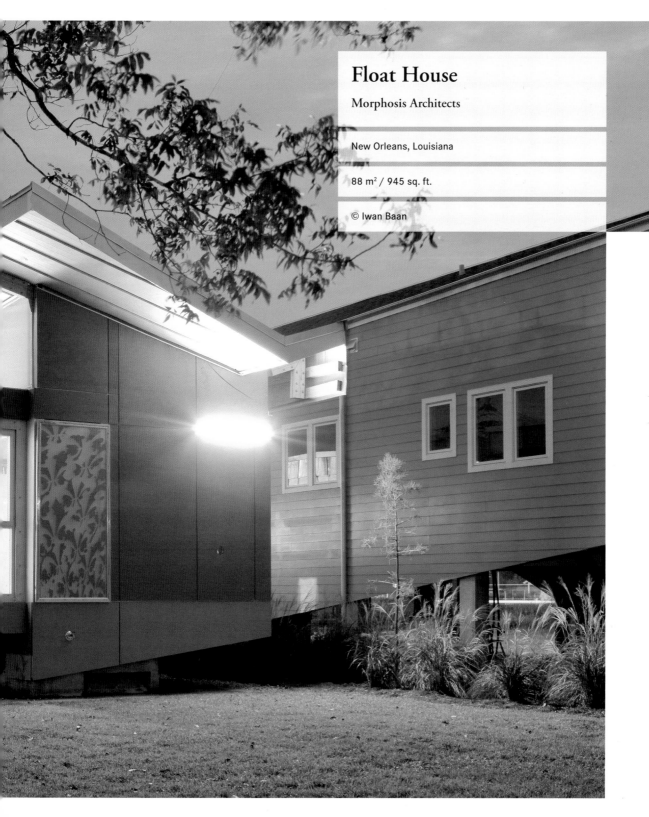

Float House

Morphosis Architects

New Orleans, Louisiana

88 m² / 945 sq. ft.

© Iwan Baan

Make It Right is an organization set up by actor Brad Pitt to help the inhabitants of New Orleans who lost their homes in the wake of Hurricane Katrina. The project this foundation undertook was to build 150 dwellings for the families of the Lower 9th Ward who were left homeless. Morphosis was one of the architectural firms invited to design an affordable, sustainable, and prefabricated prototype. This final project was the result of a collaboration between the architects, graduate students from UCLA Architecture and Urban Design, and the Clark Construction Group. The house, built as a chassis sitting on a base, is designed to withstand a hurricane as powerful as the one that devastated the city. During a flood, the chassis would float like a raft guided by steel posts. Although the owners would not be able to remain in their home, they would be able to recover it after the water receded. Solar panels provide needed electricity and the roof angle funnels rainwater for treatment and reuse. A geothermal energy system for heating and cooling and water- and energy-saving systems complete the design.

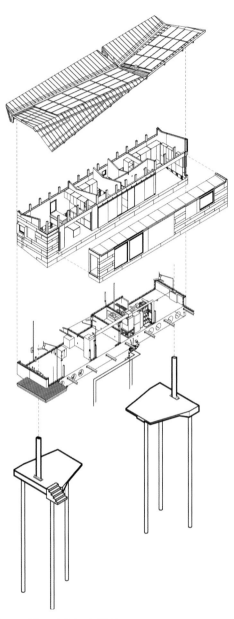

Diagram of the main features of the house

 Rainwater collection; water reuse; water-conserving fixtures

 Prefabricated construction, reducing CO_2 emissions from transportation and minimizing impact on the environment

 Photovoltaic panels; geothermal energy for heating and cooling

With the delivery of these houses in December 2010, the goal of 150 homes will be reached. They are mass-produced to make them faster to build as well as affordable.

FLOAT HOUSE: PARTS

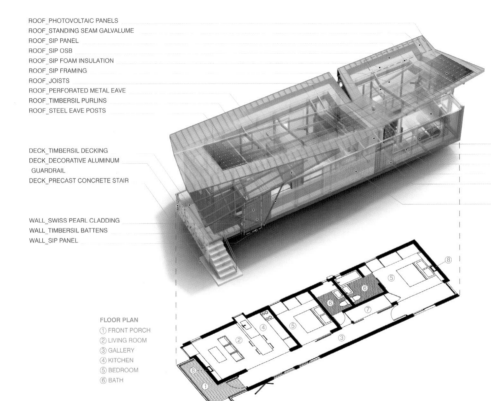

ROOF_PHOTOVOLTAIC PANELS
ROOF_STANDING SEAM GALVALUME
ROOF_SIP PANEL
ROOF_SIP OSB
ROOF_SIP FOAM INSULATION
ROOF_SIP FRAMING
ROOF_JOISTS
ROOF_PERFORATED METAL EAVE
ROOF_TIMBERSIL PURLINS
ROOF_STEEL EAVE POSTS

GALLERY_POLYCARBONATE
CLERESTORY ROOF
RAINWATER COLLECTION TANKS
GALLERY_WINDOW FRAMING
GALLERY_ STEEL DECK SUPPORTS
PHOTOVOLTAIC BATTERY STORAGE
GALLERY_POLYCARBONATE
HURRICANE SHUTTER

DECK_TIMBERSIL DECKING
DECK_DECORATIVE ALUMINUM
GUARDRAIL
DECK_PRECAST CONCRETE STAIR

WALL_SWISS PEARL CLADDING
WALL_TIMBERSIL BATTENS
WALL_SIP PANEL

FLOOR PLAN
① FRONT PORCH
② LIVING ROOM
③ GALLERY
④ KITCHEN
⑤ BEDROOM
⑥ BATH

Axonometric view and floor plan

The two double bedrooms
and two bathrooms of the
house are laid out along a
corridor. This arrangement
allows for more efficient mass
production and assembly.

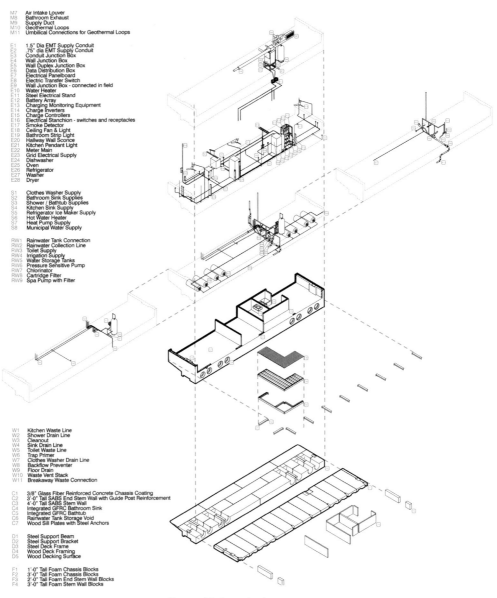

M7   Air Intake Louver
M8   Bathroom Exhaust
M9   Supply Duct
M10 Geothermal Loops
M11 Umbilical Connections for Geothermal Loops

E1   1.5" Dia EMT Supply Conduit
E2   .75" dia EMT Supply Conduit
E3   Conduit Junction Box
E4   Wall Junction Box
E5   Wall Duplex Junction Box
E6   Data Distribution Box
E7   Electrical Panelboard
E8   Electric Transfer Switch
E9   Wall Junction Box - connected in field
E10 Water Heater
E11 Steel Electrical Stand
E12 Battery Array
E13 Charging Monitoring Equipment
E14 Charge Inverters
E15 Charge Controllers
E16 Electrical Stanchion - switches and receptacles
E17 Smoke Detector
E18 Ceiling Fan & Light
E19 Bathroom Strip Light
E20 Hallway Wall Sconce
E21 Kitchen Pendant Light
E22 Meter Main
E23 Grid Electrical Supply
E24 Dishwasher
E25 Oven
E26 Refrigerator
E27 Washer
E28 Dryer

S1   Clothes Washer Supply
S2   Bathroom Sink Supplies
S3   Shower / Bathtub Supplies
S4   Kitchen Sink Supply
S5   Refrigerator Ice Maker Supply
S6   Hot Water Heater
S7   Heat Pump Supply
S8   Municipal Water Supply

RW1 Rainwater Tank Connection
RW2 Rainwater Collection Line
RW3 Toilet Supply
RW4 Irrigation Supply
RW5 Water Storage Tanks
RW6 Pressure Sensitive Pump
RW7 Chlorinator
RW8 Cartridge Filter
RW9 Spa Pump with Filter

W1   Kitchen Waste Line
W2   Shower Drain Line
W3   Cleanout
W4   Sink Drain Line
W5   Toilet Waste Line
W6   Trap Primer
W7   Clothes Washer Drain Line
W8   Backflow Preventer
W9   Floor Drain
W10 Waste Vent Stack
W11 Breakaway Waste Connection

C1   3/8" Glass Fiber Reinforced Concrete Chassis Coating
C2   3'-0" Tall SABS End Stem Wall with Guide Post Reinforcement
C3   4'-0" Tall SABS Stem Wall
C4   Integrated GFRC Bathroom Sink
C5   Integrated GFRC Bathtub
C6   Rainwater Tank Storage Void
C7   Wood Sill Plates with Steel Anchors

D1   Steel Support Beam
D2   Steel Support Bracket
D3   Steel Deck Frame
D4   Wood Deck Framing
D5   Wood Decking Surface

F1   1'-0" Tall Foam Chassis Blocks
F2   3'-0" Tall Foam Chassis Blocks
F3   2'-0" Tall Foam End Stem Wall Blocks
F4   3'-0" Tall Foam Stem Wall Blocks

Diagram of the house chassis

The architects have incorporated
a porch in the design to preserve
a tradition that has strong
roots in this area. The house is
easily accessed by both elderly
and disabled residents.

S1 4 1/2" SIPS Wall Panels
S2 Window
S3 Pop-Out Window
S4 2x2 Wood Furring Strips
S5 SwissPearl Siding

I1 Casework
I2 Sliding Interior Wood Doors
I3 Metal Sliding Door Track

G1 6 1/2" SIPS Floor Panels
G2 3/4 Subfloor
G3 Epoxy Resin Flooring
G4 4 1/2" SIPS Wall Panels
G5 4x4 Wood SIPS Post
G6 2x Wood SIPS Cap Plate
G7 Window
G8 Sliding Glass Doors
G9 2x2 Wood Furring Strips
G10 Entry Door
G11 Exposed Metal Roof Joists
G12 Polycarbonate Gallery Roof
G13 SwissPearl Siding

Diagram of wall system

Although this is the first floating
house to be permitted in the
United States, this technology
was developed in the Netherlands,
where there is a significant
demand for these kinds of
homes in towns at sea level.

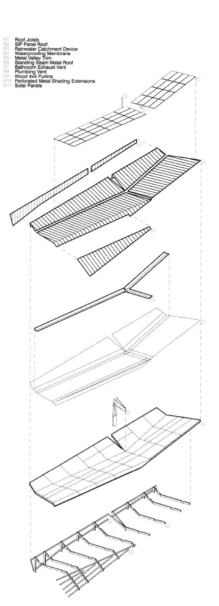

R1   Roof Joists
R2   SIP Panel Roof
R3   Rainwater Catchment Device
R4   Waterproofing Membrane
R5   Metal Valley Trim
R6   Standing Seam Metal Roof
R7   Bathroom Exhaust Vent
R8   Plumbing Vent
R9   Wood 4x4 Purlins
R10   Perforated Metal Shading Extensions
R11   Solar Panels

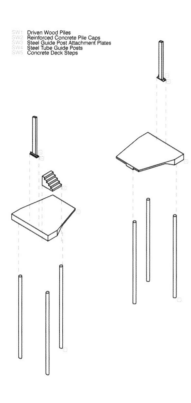

SW1   Driven Wood Piles
SW2   Reinforced Concrete Pile Caps
SW3   Steel Guide Post Attachment Plates
SW4   Steel Tube Guide Posts
SW5   Concrete Deck Steps

Exploded view of the roof and foundations of the house

A concave angle in the sloping
roof collects rainwater for filtering
and later reuse. Faucets come
with water-conserving features.

Taliesin Mod.Fab

Taliesin Design/Build Studio, Office of Mobile
Design by J. Siegal, M. P. Johnson Design Studio

Scottsdale, Arizona

89 m² / 960 sq. ft.

© Bill Timmerman

Ninety years ago, Frank Lloyd Wright introduced a pioneering plan to build houses with prefabricated parts: precut structural frames, mass-produced furnishings, etc. The First World War frustrated the project and only a handful of houses were built. The Taliesin Mod.Fab prototype is an attempt to follow in the path of the great architect and is seen as an example of a simple, elegant, and sustainable home. This home was built using structural insulated panels, which make the production and assembly processes fast and economical. It can also function off-grid, taking advantage of natural ventilation, photovoltaic panels in the garden, rainwater collection, and gray water reuse. All of these features demonstrate the feasibility of sustainable architecture that makes good use of the resources offered by nature.

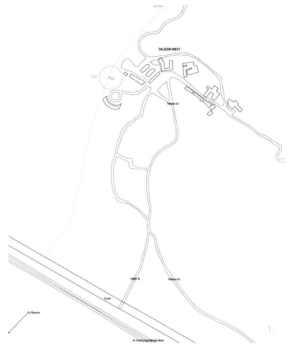

Site plan

West elevation

Rainwater collection; gray water reuse

Prefabricated parts; reducing CO_2 emissions from transportation and minimizing impact on the environment; insulated panels

Photovoltaic panels

House orientation and large windows and glass walls to make maximum use of heat and light from the sun and to provide cross ventilation

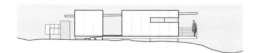

North elevation

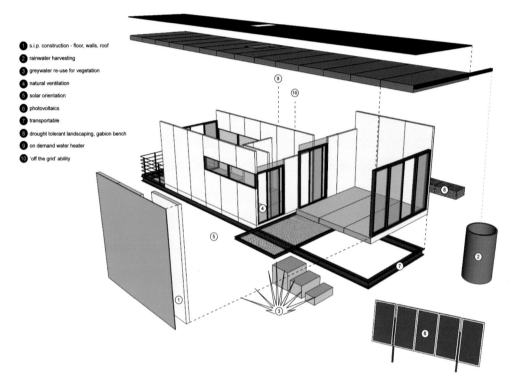

1 s.i.p. construction - floor, walls, roof
2 rainwater harvesting
3 greywater re-use for vegetation
4 natural ventilation
5 solar orientation
6 photovoltaics
7 transportable
8 drought tolerant landscaping, gabion bench
9 on demand water heater
10 'off the grid' ability

Diagram of the environmental features of the house

The photovoltaic array in the
garden provides electricity to
meet the occupants' needs.

Cross section

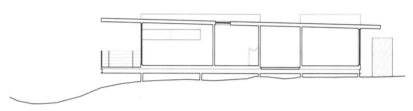

Longitudinal section

East elevation

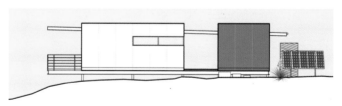

South elevation

The roof cantilever creates a
porch area that offers shelter and
shade. The glass walls let natural
light in for most of the day.

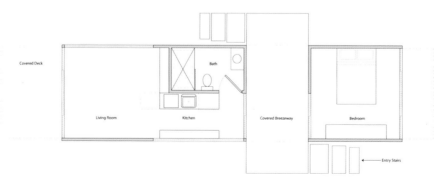

Covered Deck

Bath

Covered Breezeway

Living Room

Kitchen

Bedroom

Entry Stairs

Floor plan

House of Steel and Wood

Ecosistema Urbano Arquitectos

Ranón, Spain

90 m² / 969 sq. ft.

© Emilio P. Doiztua

This property reinterprets the traditional style of architecture typical in Asturias, a region in northern Spain. Asturian granaries are silos made of wood and raised on stilts to keep them dry, with boards to keep the rodents out. They are used mainly for storing corn, potatoes, and beans, with slits in the structure to ventilate the interior.

The building is only anchored to the ground at four points, so as to have as little impact as possible on the natural surroundings. The building itself has a compact structure and is an irregular prism on the southeastern side, allowing natural light to penetrate the building. The south side of the building is glass, and there is a sloping roof to enable the rainwater to drain off quickly. The steel and wood structure makes it easy to dismantle and recycle the building.

Longitudinal elevation

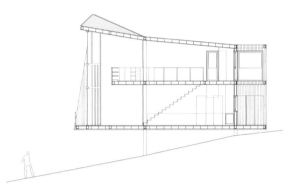

Longitudinal section

Cross elevation

 Natural and easily recyclable materials such as steel, local pine, and Douglas fir

 Angled roof oriented toward the sun and for protection against the wind

 House orientation and glass wall to make maximum use of light from the sun; sidings as natural HVAC system

 Minimal environmental impact due to building structure

The walls of the house are covered in panels of varying widths made of two types of wood, northern pine and Douglas fir. Both the orientation and geometry of the house are perfectly suited to the local climate and position of the sun.

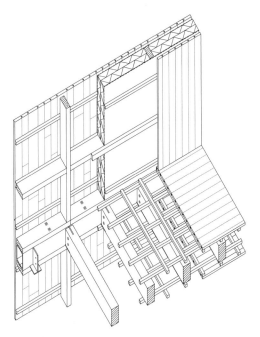

Detail of wall and slab

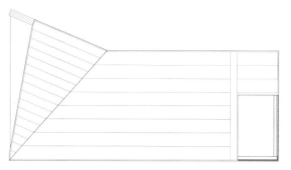

Roof

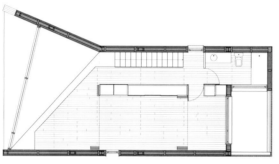

Upper floor

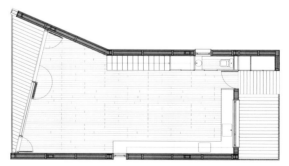

Lower floor

The property has no heating or
air-conditioning systems, since the
sidings on the outer walls, along
with the walls inside the building—
which are made of wood—prevent
the loss of heat and act as a
natural ventilation system.

itHouse

Taalman Koch Architecture

Pioneertown, California

102 m² / 1,100 sq. ft.

© Art Gray

The itHouse, designed by a team of architects with experience in combining prefab elements with on-site building methods, was engineered to minimize construction waste to the utmost. Located in the high desert region of California, the property was conceived in such a way that each client could use and arrange it to suit his or her own taste and purpose. The system allows each component of the house to arrive on the building site already cut and with directions for assembly. Only two people are required to erect the house and they can do so in a very short space of time, since the structures are small and lightweight. The house, resting on a concrete platform, consists of an aluminum frame with a steel roof and expansive glass walls. The plumbing and electrical installation conform to the specific needs of the area. The property is extremely energy efficient due to the use of passive and active systems, such as the orientation of the building, cross ventilation, the installation of low-consumption facilities, and solar panels.

Site plan

Rendering

Prefabricated materials; reusable and recyclable materials

Solar panels; radiant heating; biomass

House orientation and glass walls to make maximum use of heat and light from the sun and to provide cross ventilation

Modules built off-site to reduce CO_2 emissions from transportation and minimize the impact on the environment

The solar panels form an integral
part of the design of the house
and are installed in the central
courtyard to provide shade
during daylight hours. In winter
the house is kept warm by wood
stoves and radiant heating.

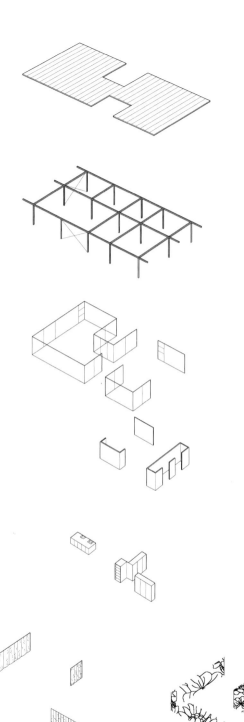

Isometric view

The architects used a graphic tool to apply vinyl pictures to the glass walls to reinforce the idea that the house is fully integrated in the desert landscape.

Sustainable House

Studio 804

Kansas City, Kansas

104 m² / 1,224 sq. ft.

© Courtesy of Studio 804

S tudio 804 is an architectural design studio where students from the University of Kansas School of Architecture and Urban Planning design a high-level sustainable project that fulfills the requirements for LEED certification for residential architecture.

This house is completely off-grid and has a multitude of features and systems that make it self-sufficient in energy and heating. The combination of passive systems, such as the glass features and the louvers that provide shade, and the active systems installed on the roof, are examples of the standards the studio pursues.

The south facade is the most exposed to the sun, enhancing the passive measures. The windows on the lower part of the south facade and the skylight in the roof produce cross ventilation. Other features are the photovoltaic panels on the roof and a domestic wind turbine, which supply the house with 100 percent of its energy requirements. Water-conserving fixtures and a system of water reuse avoid wasting this precious resource and save on water bills.

Environmental Systems Diagram

01 Photovoltaic Solar Panels	08 Steel & Glass Stair Core
02 Hydronic Radiant Floor	09 Cross Ventilation
03 Residential Wind Turbine	10 Concrete Thermal Massing
04 Geothermal Heat Pump	11 FSC Certified Tropical Wood Rainscreen
05 High Efficiency HVAC	12 High Performance Glazing System
06 Energy Recovery Ventilator (ERV)	13 Draught Tolerant Landscaping
07 Passive Solar Design	14 Rain Pervious Surfaces
	15 Rainwater Harvesting System

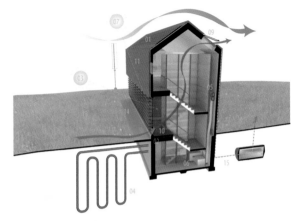

Diagram of environmental features

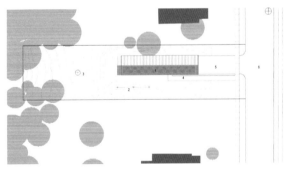

Site plan

Rainwater collection; water-conserving fixtures

Wood recycled from other buildings for interiors

Photovoltaic panels; domestic wind turbine

Natural heat and light; thermal mass; louvers to regulate the amount of light to cool the house in summer months; translucent panels surrounding the staircase to disperse light throughout the house

The wood louvers regulate
the amount of light and heat
penetrating the interior. The
electricity-producing photovoltaic
panels can be seen on the roof.

A domestic wind turbine is another
of the clean energy sources for
this home.

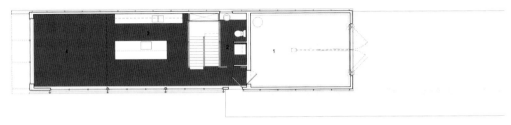

Floor plans

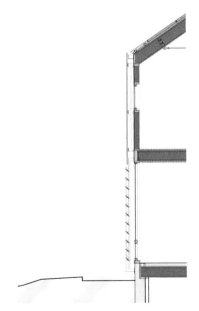

Facade construction detail

The layout of interior spaces is
like that of a conventional house:
communal areas are on the lower
level, while the bedrooms and
other spaces are upstairs.

Translucent panels surrounding
the central staircase disperse
light throughout the house. This
significantly reduces electricity
use.

A rainwater collection tank and
water-conserving faucets reduce
dependence on municipal water
and conserve a precious resource.

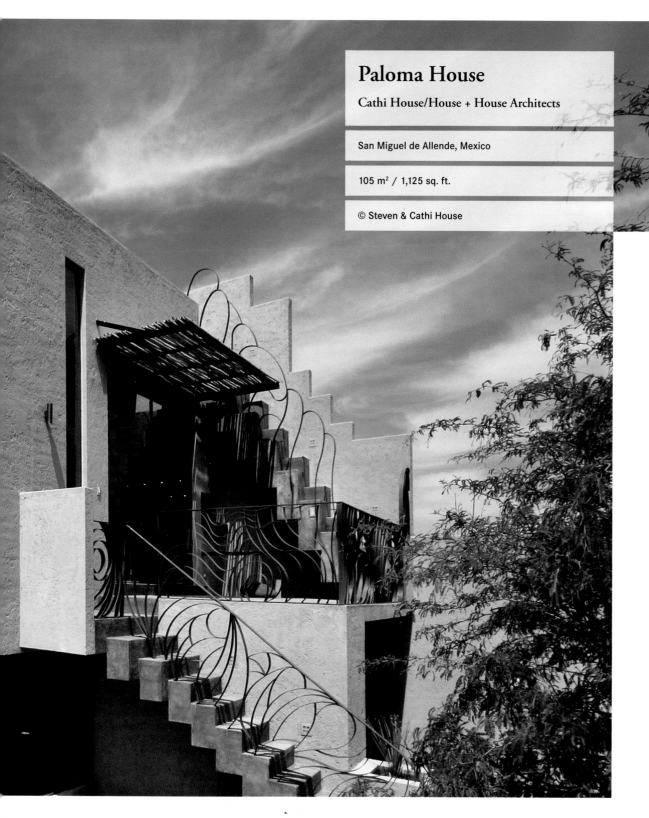

Paloma House

Cathi House/House + House Architects

San Miguel de Allende, Mexico

105 m² / 1,125 sq. ft.

© Steven & Cathi House

This small one-bedroom home is above a garage and an art studio. Three of its facades receive light. The modulation of color and light as the day progresses is accentuated by polished concrete floors, handmade tiles, and the copper of the fireplace. Sustainability was one of the criteria taken into account for the building, and different systems were designed for this purpose. The fireplace heats the whole space, and the thermal mass in the concrete floor distributes the heat captured from the sun during the day. The windows and skylights create cross ventilation and control the light entering the house to provide cooling in summer. Other systems include an on-demand gas hot water heater, LED lights, and a green roof, which helps to regulate the temperature inside the house. Rainwater collected in underground cisterns is used for watering and purified for drinking.

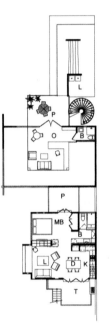

Upper and lower levels

Rainwater collection in cisterns and purification for drinking

Locally sourced materials

House orientation to make maximum use of heat and light from the sun; large windows to provide natural heat and cross ventilation; green roof; sunshades to regulate light; thermal mass

A local craftsman created the
wrought-iron banister and
local workers built the house
by hand, using materials
sourced from the area.

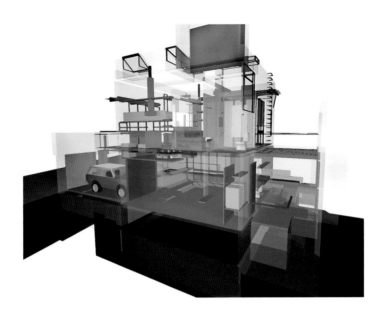

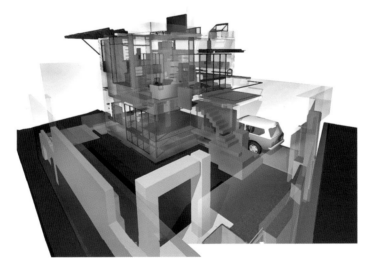

3-D renderings

A fireplace with copper
embellishment heats the single
space in winter and also separates
the bedroom from the living area,
providing a certain level of privacy.

Light entering through the window
of the sleeping area is filtered by
sunshades cantilevered from the
facade, which regulate the angle
of incidence of the sunlight.

Alpine Hut

OFIS Arhitekti

Stara Fužina, Slovenia

105 m² / 1,130 sq. ft.

© Tomaz Gregoric

This cabin is located in a small alpine village that is part of the Triglav National Park. There are very strict building rules in this area, particularly to prevent deterioration of the natural landscape. The client bought the site and existing building with the idea of making only those modifications needed for his family that would comply with certain sustainability criteria. The house, measuring 20 x 36 feet (6 x 11 m) and with a gabled roof at an angle of 42 degrees, has the same dimensions and materials as the original. The materials, including stone and timber, are locally sourced and used in a way that is consistent with the local style of architecture. The residence has a logical interior layout. The staircase wraps around the central fireplace, which provides heat for both floors. The temperature is regulated by this fireplace and passive systems, such as the windows being oriented toward the sun, and the placement of black foil behind the wood to absorb heat and conduct it to the interior. Rainwater is also collected by means of vertical pipes inserted into the wooden posts.

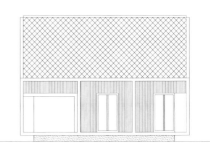

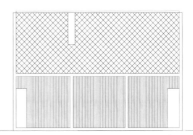

Elevations

 Rainwater collection

 Locally sourced natural materials, including stone and wood

 House orientation to make maximum use of heat from the sun; large windows to provide natural light; thick insulation; thermal mass

Composite photograph of the site

564/4

564/8

564/10

564/5

564/6

503

564/11

560

Ground plan

The slope of the roof and the
dimensions and forms of the house
are in keeping with the local style
of building and blend seamlessly
with the local architecture.

During cold and snowy weather the small porches created by the roof overhang provide for comfortable transit around the exterior of the house, which is raised slightly on pillars.

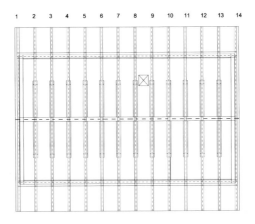

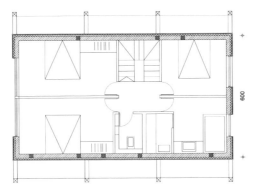

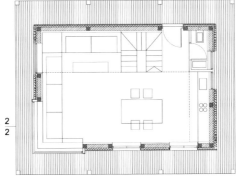

The layout of interior spaces follows a logical order. The lower level is a single space, while the upstairs landing has been all but eliminated to create bigger rooms.

Floor plans. Top to bottom: roof, upper level, and lower level

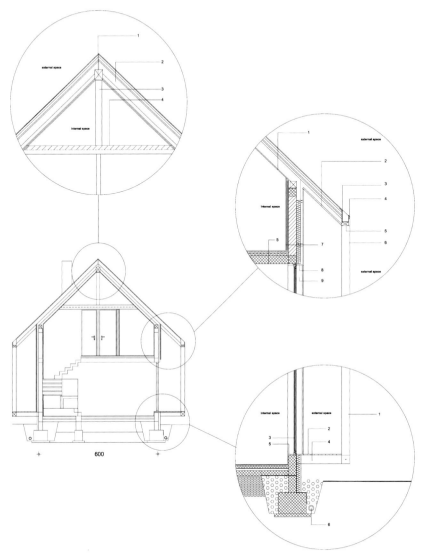

Building details: insulation

The details of the house also work
as part of its insulation, essential
to reducing electricity use and
achieving proper passive heating.

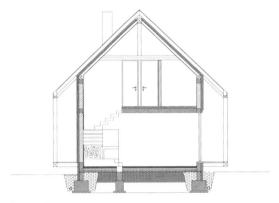

Cross section

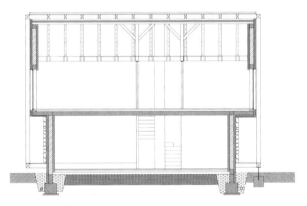

Longitudinal section

The upstairs bathroom is shared by
all of the bedrooms and features
a sauna. This project shows that
sustainability is not incompatible
with comfort and well-being.

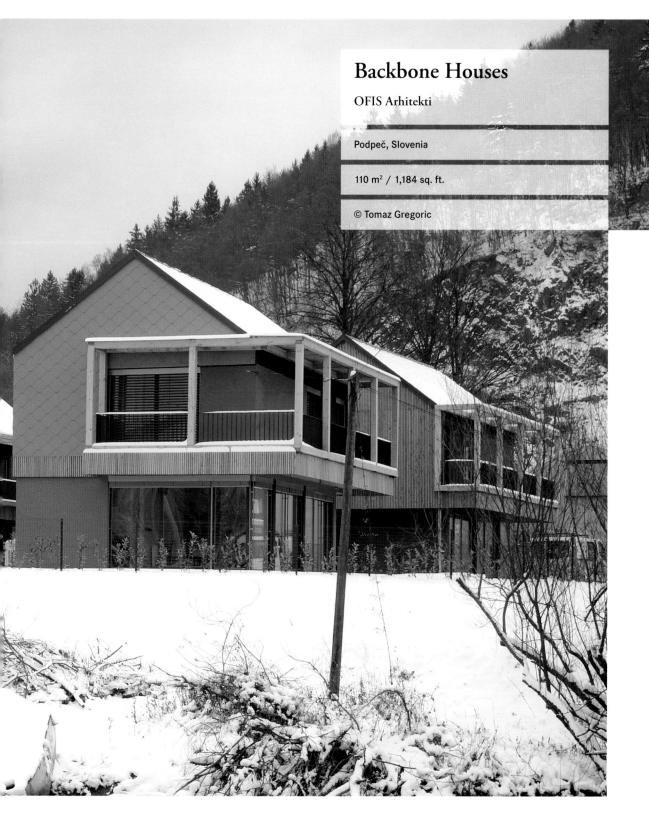

Backbone Houses

OFIS Arhitekti

Podpeč, Slovenia

110 m² / 1,184 sq. ft.

© Tomaz Gregoric

Urban growth and suburban expansion is causing the rural towns around Ljubljana to merge with the capital. At times this uncontrolled growth leads to the loss of traditional layout patterns of historic towns. This development of single-family residences in Podpeč attempts to maintain the typical layout of rural settlements with small branching streets connected by paths. The houses are designed for young families who cannot afford to live in the capital and were built with reduced budgets, basic features, and limited resources. One of the first ideas was to use the orientation of the houses and their openings to create cross ventilation. Natural light was also made use of, particularly in winter, although the overhanging features protect the interior from excess exposure to the sun in the summer. The materials are locally sourced, and the finishes are water based and nontoxic. The water used for watering the green areas is harvested rainwater.

Site plan

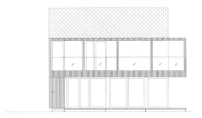

Elevations

 Rainwater collection for green areas

 Locally sourced materials; recyclable materials; water-based, nontoxic finishes

 House orientation to make maximum use of heat and light from the sun; well-positioned windows to provide natural heat, light, and cross ventilation

Composite photograph of the site

Site plan

The positioning of the houses
attempts to respect the
traditional layout of rural
settlements. A main road
connects a series of branching
paths leading to the houses.

The use of natural and recyclable
materials, such as wood,
reduce CO_2 emissions from the
manufacture of building materials.
Use of water-based paints and
varnishes reduces the presence of
chemical products in the homes.

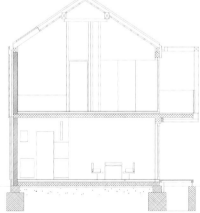

Section

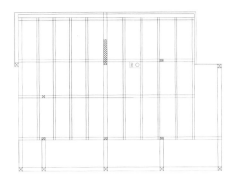

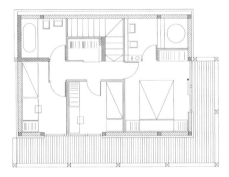

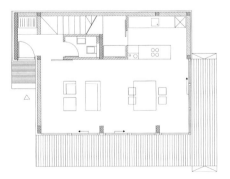

Simplicity of design is a formula for achieving sustainable architecture. The proper layout of interior spaces can lead to improved heating, ventilation, and lighting.

Floor plans. Top to bottom: roof, upper level, and lower level

Bridge House

Max Pritchard Architect

Ashbourne, Australia

110 m² / 1,184 sq. ft.

© Sam Noonan

The clients' brief was for a home and office. It needed to take into account the sloping bank of a creek that crossed the property without spoiling the natural beauty of the site. The architects adapted their design to a reduced budget, comparable to that for a prefabricated house. The result was a rectangular building bridging the stream. A steel frame was anchored at four points with concrete piers. This structure supports a concrete floor slab on which the house, measuring just over 1,000 square feet (100 m²), stands. The structure and shape of the house reduce its carbon footprint on the land. The two main facades face north and south, an orientation that allows for comfortable temperatures in all seasons; the black concrete on the floor stores heat through thermal mass, and this heat is retained by means of double-paned windows. Steel cladding and the trees surrounding the house protect from the high temperatures of the summer months. Other ecological features of this house are locally sourced and recycled materials and the solar panels that heat water and provide electricity.

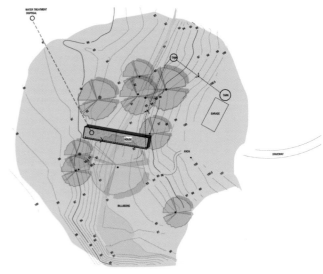

Site plan

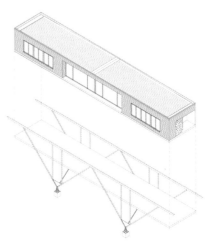

Axonometric view of the structure

 Rainwater collection for domestic use

 Locally sourced and recycled materials

 Solar panels for hot water and electricity

 House orientation to make maximum use of heat and light from the sun and cross ventilation; thermal mass; double-paned windows for insulation; trees for shade in summer

 Minimal environmental impact due to metal structure

Because the house is built over a
metal structure, it has minimum
impact on the site, given that there
was no need to cut down trees or
change the course of the stream.

In winter, the double-paned
windows keep in the heat entering
through the north facade.
In the southern hemisphere,
the sun crosses the sky from
east to west to the north.

Floor plan

Lavaflow 3

Craig Steely Architecture

Big Island, Hawaii

21 + 74 m² / 1,300 + 800 sq. ft. (house + terraces)

© Cesar Rubio

This magnificent house was built at a distance of only 10 miles (16 km) from Mount Kilauea, one of several active volcanoes on the largest of the Hawaiian Islands. Located above the only black sand beach on the island, it occupies only 2,100 square feet (200 m²), giving it a human scale in the midst of a natural setting. The orientation of the house is one of the architect's success stories: in addition to affording ocean views from all of the windows, it also takes full advantage of breezes, making air-conditioning unnecessary. A series of curtains, screens, and louvers regulate the breezes like the sails of a ship and also regulate the entry of light into the house and protect the privacy of its occupants. In a delicate and sensitive volcanic environment, the sustainability of any buildings is essential. All of the water used in the house comes from rainwater collected and stored in a concrete cistern under the timber floor in the living area.

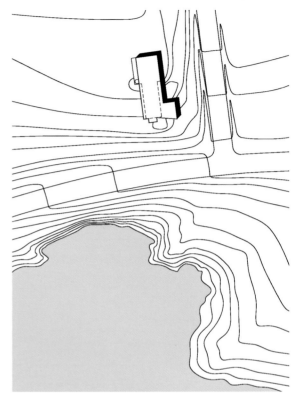

Site plan

 Rainwater collection on the roof and storage under the house

 House orientation to provide cross ventilation; large windows to provide natural light; a system of curtains, screens, and louvers to regulate breezes and light

 Minimal environmental impact due to the pillars supporting the house

The house was built on pillars, reducing the impact of construction on the delicate volcanic soil. The windows and decks allow the impressive views to be enjoyed.

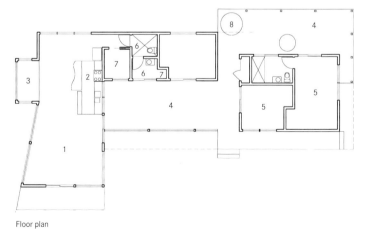

Floor plan

1. Living area
2. Kitchen
3. Deck
4. Outdoor area
5. Bedroom
6. Bathroom
7. Storage space
8. Tree well

The wood louvers serve to regulate
the temperature and the amount
of daylight entering the house.
Such extensive use of natural light
reduces electricity consumption.

Lake Seymour Getaway

UCArchitect

Marmora, Canada

122 m² / 1,315 sq. ft.

© UCArchitect

This vacation house is located near the city of Peterborough, halfway between Toronto and Ottawa. The architects from UCArchitect concentrated on sustainability and the surroundings when designing this retreat. Sustainability strategies are implemented through cross ventilation, radiant heating, reinforced insulation, and passive solar energy. The property has spectacular views of the lake and groves of pine and cedar trees surrounding the area.

An L-shaped wooden screen marks the entrance and generates a wraparound deck on the outside of the building. An important relationship has been created between the interior and exterior of the house, which is accentuated by the existence of skylights, roof overhangs, and large openings instead of traditional windows.

The inside of the house has been designed around the central area occupied by the kitchen and bathroom. The various parts of the house are only separated by three sliding doors, designed to connect the spaces in a number of different ways.

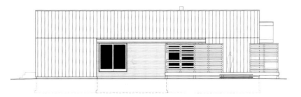

Elevation 1

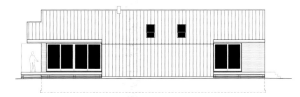

Elevation 2

Recyclable and reusable materials such as cedar; low-maintenance materials such as concrete

Rotating oven

Skylights and large windows to provide natural light and cross ventilation; radiant heating

Minimal environmental impact due to the design of the building; preservation of local vegetation

Large windows are installed to
enable the maximum amount
of natural light to penetrate
the building. Timber is used for the
facade and entrances to the house.

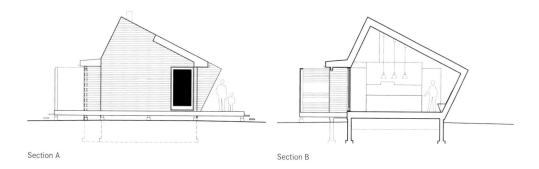

Section A

Section B

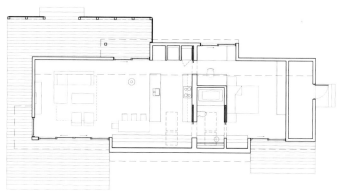

Floor plan

The interior features a minimalist style that exploits the dimensions of the space to the utmost. A fully rotating oven, installed on a concrete pillar in the middle of the house, takes center stage.

Glass & Timber Houses

Hampson Williams

London, United Kingdom

130 m²; 140 m² / 1,399 sq. ft.; 1,507 sq. ft.

© Tim Soar

Following the demolition of some old workshops inside a residential complex, two new terraced houses were erected, both featuring finely detailed joinery. The design is characterized by a smart planimetric shape that combines compact wooden forms with open spaces and glass. The client was a joiner who was extremely proud of his work and wanted his new home to showcase his trade. Each house is arranged around an inner courtyard with a ground plan that is formed around an irregularly shaped site, allowing gardens to be planted on each corner. The construction of this inner courtyard sheds a great deal of natural light, which is filtered through the double-height glass windows. Enhancing the cedarwood interiors, large floor-to-ceiling glass walls have been put in, affording views of the inner courtyard and some of the surrounding area outside. Biodiversity has been enhanced with the creation of perfect nesting sites for birdlife and insects.

Site plan

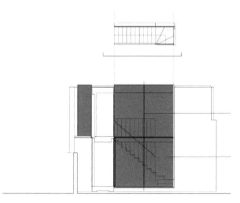

Detail of the section of the staircase

 Rainwater collection on the roof for watering the garden

 Natural materials that form part of the surroundings

 House orientation, inner courtyard, and large windows and glass walls to make maximum use of heat and light from the sun and to provide cross ventilation; wooden planks for insulation

Wooden planks of red cedar
are used as wall cladding
and offer excellent thermal
insulation, translating into
low energy consumption.

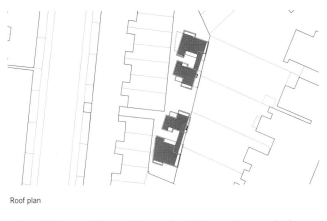

Roof plan

Upper floor

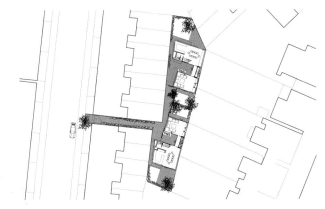

Lower floor

Sections

Inside, the different spaces are separated by glass partitions running from floor to ceiling, which allow natural light to penetrate all communal areas.

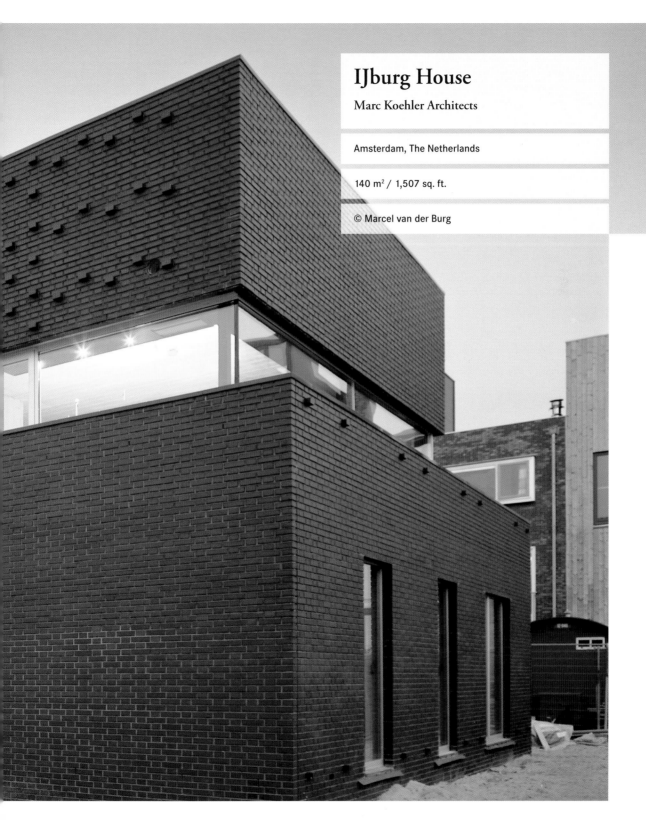

IJburg House

Marc Koehler Architects

Amsterdam, The Netherlands

140 m² / 1,507 sq. ft.

© Marcel van der Burg

The house was built on a small plot of land in IJburg, a recently developed suburb of the city of Amsterdam. It was designed as a monolithic sculpture, displaying a contrast between the closed private spaces and the communal areas, which seem to have been carved out of a solid block. The property looks as if it has been designed as a vertical garden. Aesthetically, the architecture is connected visually to the street, garden, and terrace on the 775-square-foot (72 m²) roof. The house has two different levels: the upper story is divided into three bedrooms, a small bathroom, and a multipurpose area, and the lower level is occupied by the kitchen and dining area. The living room, which can be used for various purposes, leads out to the garden located at the back of the house. This same space also includes an artist's studio, a worktable, and a small play area. The property features a wall of brick masonry, a technique originating in the famous Amsterdam School during the 1920s.

Concept drawings

 Low-maintenance materials; recyclable bricks

 "Natural curtain" of vegetation to provide shade; large windows to provide natural heat and cross ventilation

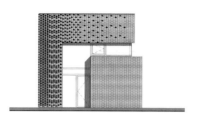

North elevation

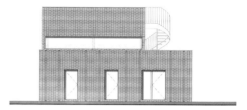

West elevation

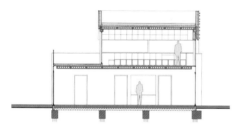

Section A

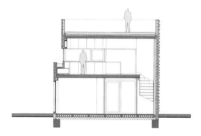

Section B

The front brickwork has specific details suggestive of the techniques created by the famous Amsterdam School in the 1920s. This material has a long life, no maintenance costs, and can be recycled.

This original construction at the front means that certain plant species, such as ivy, vines, and roses, will shortly be able to climb up the wall and create a natural curtain providing shade and privacy.

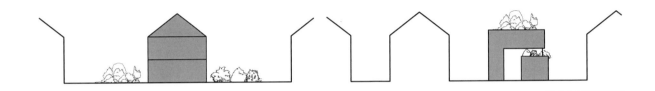

Roof garden

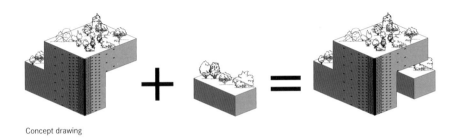

Concept drawing

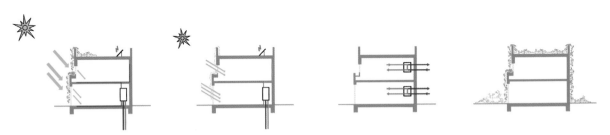

Drawings showing energy sufficiency

Large windows were incorporated
to capture the maximum amount of
natural light and to warm the inside
of the house without the need
for an artificial heating system.

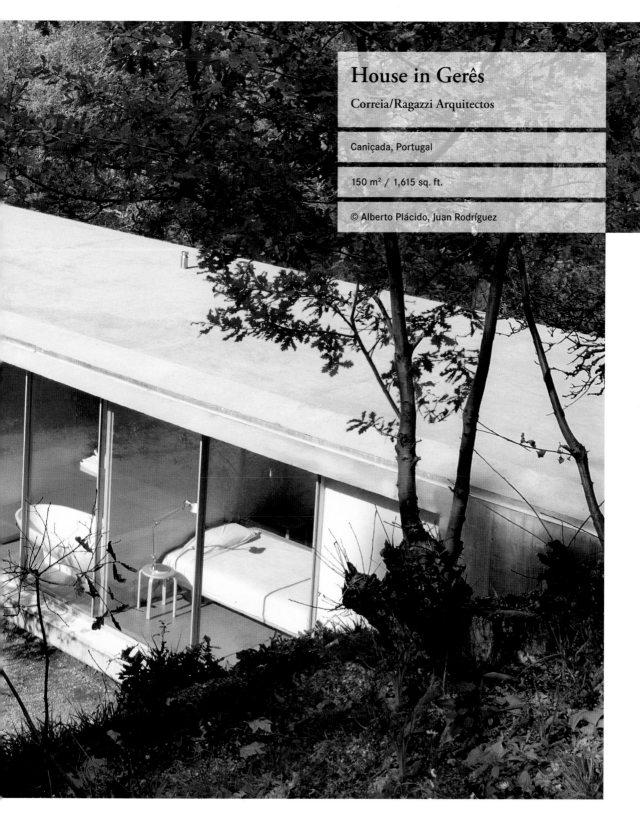

House in Gerês

Correia/Ragazzi Arquitectos

Caniçada, Portugal

150 m² / 1,615 sq. ft.

© Alberto Plácido, Juan Rodríguez

The site where the house was to be located presented a number of limitations, including a very steep slope and the need to keep intact a large expanse of woodland. The first problem was solved with the decision to anchor the building to the ground, and the second obstacle was overcome by creating a narrow cantilever leading down to the river. This project involved the reconstruction of an old dry-stone building and the construction of a new structure on a site located in a protected natural area. The clients wanted to have a weekend home where they could relax and their child could play in natural surroundings. The architects' main aim was to design a building that would enable the residents to enjoy the exceptional views the place had to offer. To that end, they created spaces that, instead of opening out onto the landscape, seem to be an integral part of it. The result of their in-depth study of the task at hand led to the construction of a single volume of reinforced concrete in the shape of a prism facing the river, designed in such a way that it would occupy a very small plot of land.

Site plan

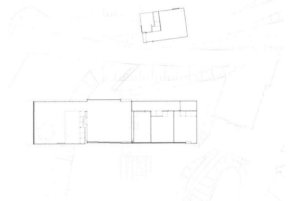

Floor plan

 Water-saving faucets

 Reused materials; natural materials with low environmental impact

 Glass walls to provide natural heat and cross ventilation

 Low environmental impact due to the design of the building

North elevation

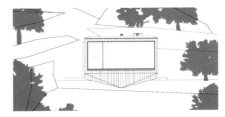

Section D-D

South elevation

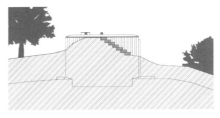

Section E-E

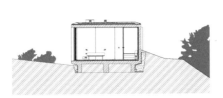

West elevation

Section I-I

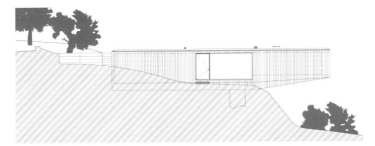

Section J-J

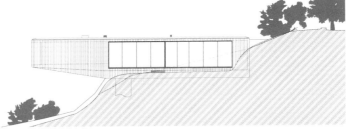

Section L-L

The sidewalls of the prism are predominantly glass, with windows reaching from floor to ceiling, affording panoramic views of the countryside.

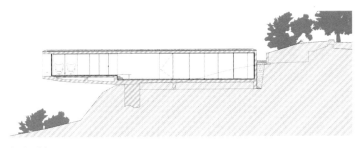

Section B-B

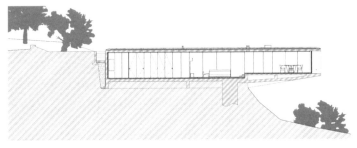

Section A-A

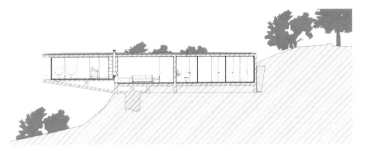

Section C-C

The volume of reinforced concrete
protrudes beyond the cliff, thanks
to the installation of a platform at
its base. As the house was built
on a slope, the only horizontal
surface is inside the building.

Both the interiors using elements
from an old stone building
and the newly built areas are
austere and minimalist in design.
Natural materials have been
used to clad the building.

Residential Containers

Petr Hájek Architekti

Prague, Czech Republic

151 m² / 1,625 sq. ft.

© Ester Havlova

Remodeling projects can be increasingly seen as exercises in passive architecture or sustainable architecture. The need to remodel a home can be an excuse to include energy-saving features and recyclable or natural materials. There are a number of examples in this project. This addition was made with two shipping containers wedged into the roof of a building in Prague. The new spaces contain living areas while the old attics were turned into bedrooms and dressing rooms. Glass expanses provide natural light for the entire home and also allow the sun to heat the rooms. An electronic system controls the amount of sunlight entering the apartment and regulates the temperature by automatically raising or lowering the sunshades. No other type of heating is necessary with this system, achieving significant energy savings.

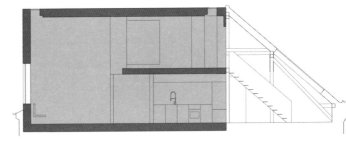

Section

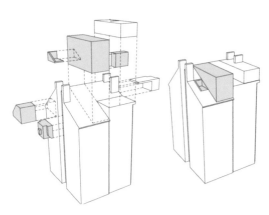

Axonometric view of the inserted containers

 Repurposed containers as living spaces; attic remodeling with traditional systems and materials

 Large windows to provide cross ventilation; electronic sunshades to regulate heat and light; absence of partitions to allow light to penetrate the entire home; interiors painted pale colors to reflect light

The shipping containers blend
seamlessly with the building.
The large windows provide the
apartment with light and heat.

The apartment interior has
two interconnected levels.
The absence of partition walls
allows light to penetrate the
entire home and stabilizes the
temperature throughout.

The interiors were painted pale colors to enhance available daylight. Central Europe does not enjoy many hours of sun, so it was necessary to adopt these kinds of strategies to reduce the need for use of artificial light.

The warmth of wood contrasts
with the metal sunshades
controlling the entry of light
and heat into the apartment.

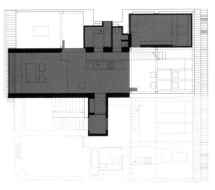

Lower level

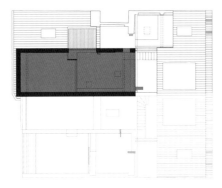

Loft space

The loft space created in the
apartment features a small
and comfortable reading room
with views of the exterior
and the lower level.

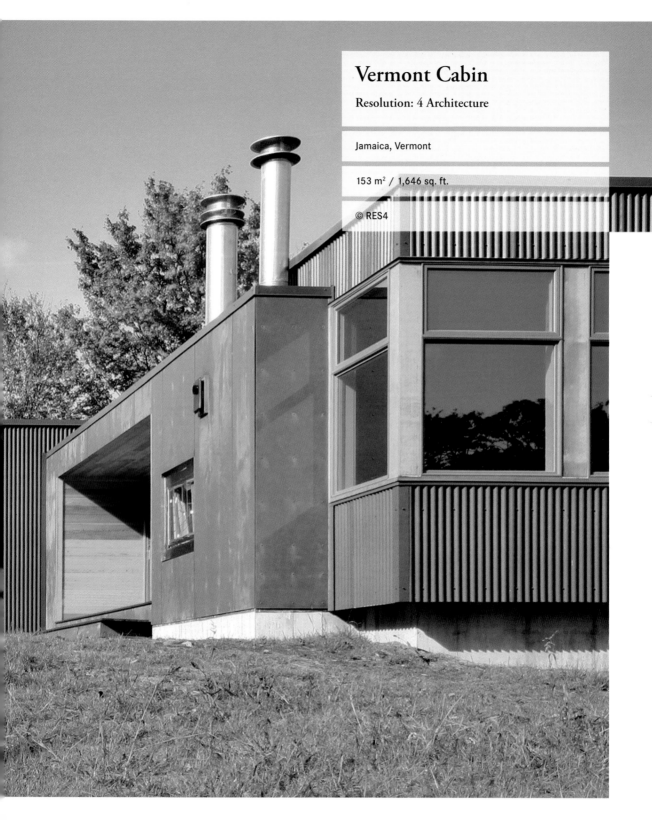

Vermont Cabin

Resolution: 4 Architecture

Jamaica, Vermont

153 m² / 1,646 sq. ft.

© RES4

This prefabricated house is located in a small town in the state of Vermont. Nearby is a state park crossed by the West River and Hamilton Falls. Prefabricated houses involve less impact on the land and lower CO_2 emissions as building times are shorter. Here, a concrete base was built on which factory-made modules were positioned. The house is off-grid; any electricity required is produced by photovoltaic panels. Radiant floor heating keeps the house warm in the coldest months. Different types of materials were used: recyclable materials, such as the corrugated-metal cladding, and other natural materials, such as the cedar used on the exterior and the bamboo flooring inside the house. The result is a house that blends noninvasively with its surroundings and provides a genuine experience of coexistence with nature.

Floor plan

 Recyclable and natural materials such as corrugated-metal cladding and bamboo; insulated glass

 Photovoltaic panels; radiant heating

 Prefabricated modules and short on-site construction to reduce CO_2 emissions from transportation and minimize impact on the environment

The house stands in a small clearing where it receives direct sunlight. A road through an adjoining forest connects the house with the nearest town.

Prefabricated construction
involves lower impact on the
environment. The building time
and the presence of machinery
and workers are reduced from
months to weeks, to even days.

The layout of the house is very simple: an open-plan kitchen and living-dining area, two bathrooms and three bedrooms—one of which is used for several purposes.

House 205

H Arquitectes

Vacarisses, Spain

57 m² / 1,690 sq. ft.

© Starp Estudi

At first sight, the steeply sloping, craggy terrain covered in pine trees and buried in undergrowth did not look at all promising as a potential site for the house. The architects intended to avoid altering the environment and to maximize the character of the place. Thus, they removed the first layer of earth and exposed a large bed of rock on which to locate the house without damaging the surroundings. The existing natural layout was used to provide entry to and exit from the garden, which at the same time conserved the features of the forest and its flora. The only artificial changes made were the adjustment of the access road and the construction of the house, which was designed in keeping with criteria espousing sustainability and a low impact on the environment. The structure is composed of laminated timber and load-bearing walls with a lightweight truss system incorporating large KLH paneling. This system behaves like a huge beam, reducing CO_2 emissions and water usage associated with the construction of a foundation.

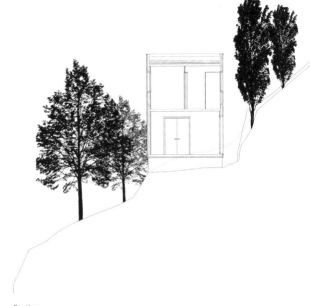

Section

Section

Recyclable materials such as laminated wood

Windows to provide natural light and cross ventilation; shutters to regulate light

Minimal environmental impact due to the use of load-bearing walls and a lightweight truss system rather than construction of a concrete foundation

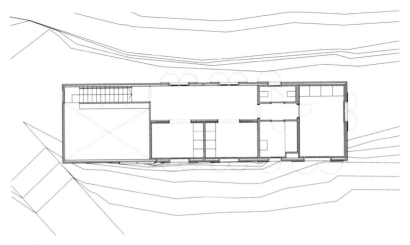

Upper floor

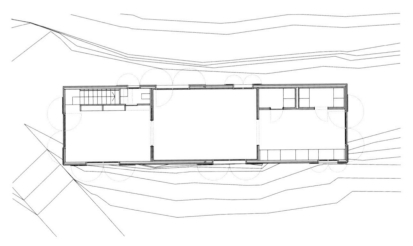

Lower floor

Flemish pine was used for
the cladding on the facade,
and the openings made in the
structure also have wooden
shutters and frames.

The most important material featured in this construction is laminated wood, which is used both in the interior and on the exterior, and can be dismantled and reused.

Brooks Ave. House Addition

Bricault Design

Los Angeles, California

158 m² / 1,700 sq. ft.

© Kenji Arai, Richard Grisby

The clients were in need of more space in their home but were reluctant to leave the area. They finally decided to extend their existing house. This new addition occupies the rear of the lot. The region has a mild climate for most of the year, and priority was given to ecological features that would provide temperature comfort, electricity, and efficient water use. A sculptural central staircase links the three different levels of the house and pivoting doors connect the house with the courtyard, allowing cross ventilation and making air-conditioning unnecessary. The green roof, also featuring a vegetable garden, is watered with rainwater and recycled gray water. The roof of the original house has a photovoltaic panel array to produce electricity. A high-efficiency boiler saves energy and supplies hot water and heating. Low-flow toilets and nontoxic paints and varnishes are also features.

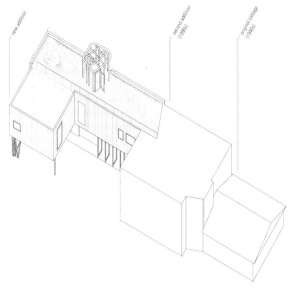

Axonometric view of the addition

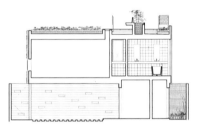

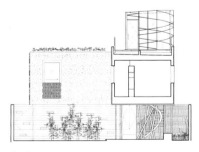

Sections

 Use of rainwater and recycled gray water for green roof and garden; low-flow toilets

 Cork floors and recycled cotton-fiber insulation; nontoxic paints and varnishes

 Photovoltaic panels; LED lights; energy-efficient boiler

 Central staircase and pivoting doors to allow cross ventilation; green roof

The California climate is mild
for most of the year. Cross
ventilation and a green roof
are ecological and economical
solutions for cooling the house.

The green roof helps to regulate
the interior temperature. Rainwater
and previously filtered gray water
are used to prevent using more
potable water than is necessary.

The central staircase and pivoting
doors are the primary built
features that provide the house
with cross ventilation, allowing
a breeze to cool the interior.

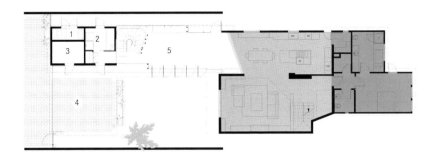

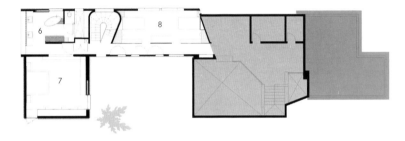

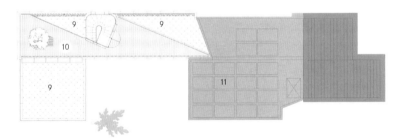

Floor plans

1. Systems
2. Laundry
3. Storage space
4. Garage
5. Main entrance
6. Master bathroom

7. Master bedroom
8. Bedroom
9. Vegetable garden
10. Green roof
11. Photovoltaic panels

This addition is not the first this house has seen. The original 1940s house had previously been extended in the 1990s.

Restored Farmhouse

Jeffrey McKean Architect

Claryville, New York

159 m² / 1,710 sq. ft.

© Keith Mendenhall/Jeffrey McKean Architect

This 1848 farmhouse built from hemlock wood was in a very bad state and in need of urgent action. The restoration of the farmhouse and the building of an addition were the basis of the project by the Jeffrey McKean practice. The addition is a simple rectilinear volume clad in recycled timber and FSC-certified cedar. The rough wood siding is vertical to contrast with the well-finished horizontal siding of the original farmhouse. With the passing of time, the two surfaces will take on a more uniform appearance, which will cause the two volumes to blend visually. The addition has a frame made of glued laminated timber (glulam) and structural insulated panels (SIPs). The glass also features a high degree of insulation. The placement of the windows of the farmhouse and the addition produce good cross ventilation, and the double-height windows let plenty of light enter the house. The varnishes and paints used to restore the timber and floors have low volatile organic compound (VOC) levels.

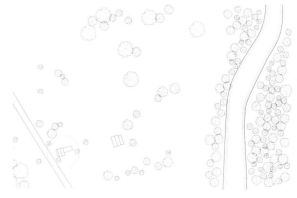

Site plan

Longitudinal section

Cross section

Recycled and natural materials such as timber; FSC-certified wood; glulam frame; insulated panels and glass; low-VOC paints and varnishes

Energy-efficient appliances

Well-positioned, large windows to provide natural light and cross ventilation

The owner of the farm is also the
owner of the adjoining property,
known as ModestHouse, which
he plans to turn into a hybrid,
sustainable house based on the
same principles as those governing
the restoration of the farmhouse.

The contrast between the siding
of the old farmhouse and the
addition will be reduced with
time as atmospheric conditions
act on both surfaces.

North elevation

East elevation

South elevation

West elevation

The restoration of wood
and the use of FSC-certified
timber guarantee that natural
resources are not wasted.
Cost savings are achieved
and deforestation is halted.

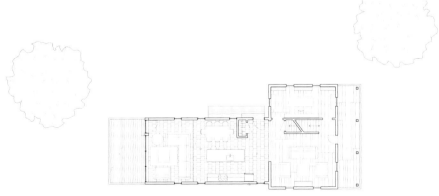

Lower level

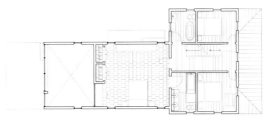

Upper level

Lockyer Residence

Shaun Lockyer Architects, Arkhefield

Brisbane, Australia

160 m² / 1,722 sq. ft.

© Scott Burrows

This project consists of an addition to an older house owned by a young family to provide needed flexibility with a view to future changes in the family. It was also an attempt to enhance contact with the external landscape and take further advantage of the breezes in the area and the hours of daylight. The older building did not have a good orientation. A study was made of how to best use openings and the location of the new spaces to achieve cross ventilation and natural heating and cooling. A minimum of materials was employed; even material from the construction work was incorporated. Most of the wood is FSC certified. The mix of architectural styles from two different periods preserves local traditions while adding modernity to the neighborhood. The block, with its glass expanses, lights up at night like a lighthouse in the street.

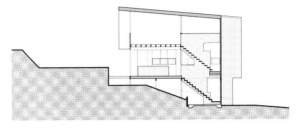

Cross section

Longitudinal section

Cross section

 Reuse of materials from the building work; FSC-certified wood

 House orientation and well-positioned windows to make maximum use of heat and light from the sun and to provide cross ventilation; glass walls to provide natural light; porch canopy for shade

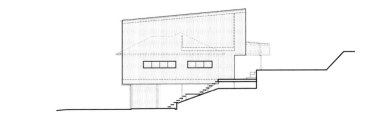

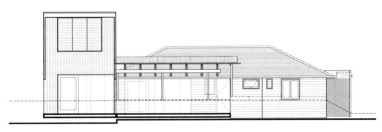

Elevations

The glass expanse of the addition allows natural light to enter during the day and makes outdoor lighting unnecessary—this new structure also illuminates part of the street.

The porch canopy has an exposed frame and materials. This feature provides shade in summer and shelter from rain. The sliding glass wall connects the interior with the exterior.

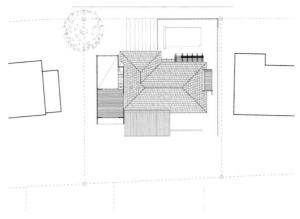

Roof plan

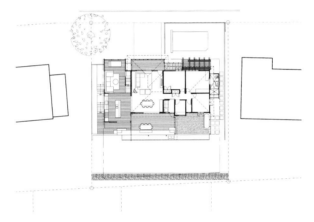

Upper level

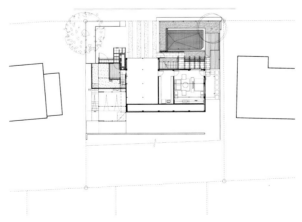

Lower level

The orientation of the new rooms takes advantage of the benefits of both cross ventilation and heat from the sun. The living area has the best light in the house.

Sebastopol Residence

Turnbull Griffin Haesloop

Sebastopol, California

167 m² / 1,800 sq. ft. (main house)

© David Wakely

This house, set between two stands of redwoods, was designed for two graphic designers. The north facade features a glass expanse that covers almost the entire length of the house, enabling the occupants to enjoy the splendid views of the mountain landscape. The good natural lighting achieved by this insulated glass wall reduces the need for excessive use of electricity during the day. A string of clerestory windows on the south facade captures the sun's heat and achieves a certain amount of passive heat during the winter. During the summer months, the redwoods provide considerable shade, both preventing the house from overheating and enhancing cross ventilation. Interior and exterior make extensive use of natural materials. The rooms of the house are laid out the length of the rectangular floor plan. The living area and master bedroom occupy the ends, both with direct access to the outside. The central area is where the kitchen, a study, and the master bathroom are located. Additional spaces complete the design.

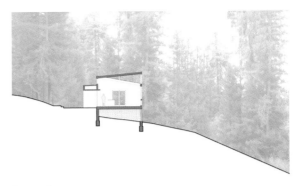

Cross section

Site plan

Natural and easily recycled materials

Solar panels to heat the swimming pool; biomass stove

House orientation to make maximum use of heat and light from the sun; large windows and glass wall to provide natural heat; trees to provide shade in the summer

The redwoods and the other
trees protect the house from
high summer temperatures.
Shade is one of the most
effective passive systems. It also
enhances cross ventilation.

Solar panels heat the water in
the swimming pool. As the pool's
use is limited to the months
of warm weather, excessive
energy use is avoided.

Floor plan

The large expanses of glass
on the north facade and part
of the south facade let light
in throughout the day.

Seadrift Residence

CCS Architecture

Stinson Beach, California

176.5 m² / 1,900 sq. ft.

© Mathew Millman

CS Architecture designed this sustainable property as a second home for three generations of the same family from San Francisco. Seadrift was erected in the 1950s, in the area around Stinson Beach, a neighborhood of vacation homes for wealthy families. The design of this property followed a rigorous sustainability program and included the installation of photovoltaic panels. All the home's systems—hot water, HVAC, and radiant heating—are integrated in a power grid that runs on solar energy. The only gas available is in the kitchen, where it is piped in from a propane tank. Apart from this one exception, the house has net-zero energy consumption. The strict building codes in the area meant that the architects had to design the structure like a pier. The living area is in the center, with the outdoor areas arranged around it. The house is divided into two sectors: the bedrooms occupy one wing, and the communal areas (living room, kitchen, dining room, and multipurpose space) occupy the other.

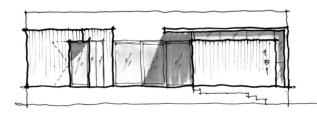

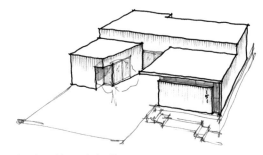

Drawings of the south elevation

Recyclable and reusable natural materials, including wood, glass, and aluminum

Photovoltaic panels; biomass

Skylights and large windows to provide natural light and cross ventilation

Glass railings allow
uninterrupted views of the
water and surrounding hills.

Floor plan

With its open-plan layout, this home has been designed to accommodate a large number of people. The living area opens out onto large wooden decks.

The living area opens onto an inner
courtyard on the southern side and
a deck on the lagoon side. The
Fireorb in the living area may
be rotated to heat the house or
radiate warmth to the deck.

House in Hattem

Arconiko Architecten

Hattem, The Netherlands

180 m² / 1,937 sq. ft.

© Luuk Kramer

This property, with its original construction and design, is located on the edge of the old part of Hattem. The architects were commissioned to renovate a house dating back to 1900 to enhance its wonderful views of the river and town. The architectural firm also decided to apply the concepts of sustainability to their design.

One of the most prominent features of the renovation is the creation of a volume with a facade that incorporates continuous, curved wooden beams. The existing spaces that have been salvaged are the garage, foundation, cellar, and east-facing wall.

The most important task was to design spaces that would maximize the available sunlight. Hence, in the communal or social areas, such as the living room and kitchen, the facade faces south and is fully glassed in. In keeping with this leitmotif, strategic openings have been made on the north side to install skylights, which bring natural light into the darkest corners of the house.

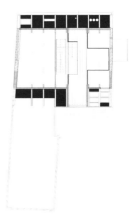

Top floor

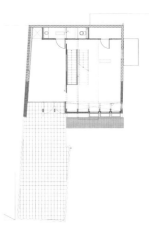

Middle floor

First floor

 Locally sourced materials

 Low energy consumption

 House orientation, skylights, and windows to make maximum use of heat and light from the sun and to provide cross ventilation; thermal mass

The use of local materials, such as timber, in the main structure, roof, profiles, and stairway, is one of the most important sustainable aspects of this property.

The architects decided to focus their attention on creating bright areas in the house by installing skylights that allow natural light to flow into the house.

Annie Residence

Bercy Chen Studio

Austin, Texas

86 m² / 2,000 sq. ft.

© Mike Osborne, Joseph Pettyjohn

This home consists of two pavilions connected by a glass hallway framing a water feature. The architects wished to show through this design that there is no reason why sustainable architecture should be divorced from its surroundings. Each pavilion has a central core, made of a steel frame covered with red or blue acrylic panels.

The steel of the frame module, recyclable, is combined with ThermaSteel panels. This prefabricated system reduces material and building costs. The panels, in combination with concrete floors and double-paned glass, provide exceptional insulation for the house. It was essential to achieve a high level of insulation efficiency in a setting with considerable solar incidence.

The rooms are laid out around a central courtyard. The internal partitions can be moved and opened, allowing the entire house to be cooled by cross ventilation. A nearby deciduous tree offers shade in summer and lets light into the house in winter.

Roof plan

Lower level

 Rainwater collection for watering; low-maintenance, drought-resistant native plants

 Recyclable steel in frame; natural materials such as glass and steel; insulated ThermaSteel panels; prefabricated modules; double-paned glass

 Photovoltaic panels

 Concrete and double-paned, insulated, and tinted glass to provide insulation; partitions to facilitate cross ventilation; overhangs and vegetation to cool the house

Tress and plants are passive
cooling systems for houses. Plants
help to cool and purify the air.
Deciduous trees provide shade in
summer and sun in winter.

The glazing consists of double-pane, insulated, tinted glass, which shields the interior from excessive heat from the sun.

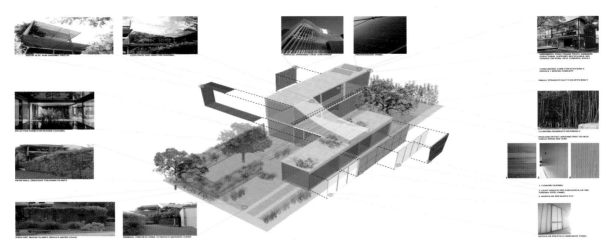

Diagram of environmental features

The diagram shows the location of the different features contributing to make the house sustainable, with reduced water and energy use.

The design of the house is
influenced by the architecture of
other regions. The transparency
of the volumes and the minimalist
interior are inspired by Japanese
pavilions.

Peconic Bay House

Resolution: 4 Architecture

Shinnecock Hills, New York

186 m² / 2,004 sq. ft.

© RES4

T his prefabricated house combination was designed as the best solution for a three-bedroom, two-bathroom house. The main volume is protected by warm-hued cedarwood while another part of the exterior is covered in cement. The home is located on an elevated part of the site to give it views of the bay. The photovoltaic panels on the roof and the use of geothermal energy turn the house into a power plant that also supplies the local grid daily.

The sustainability of this home is determined by a number of features: The company that manufactured the prefabricated pieces has its own waste management and material recycling programs. Prefab construction requires shorter work times, which lessens the environmental impact on the site. Plantings do not include nonnative varieties, the lawn area is limited, and drought-resistant plants have been used.

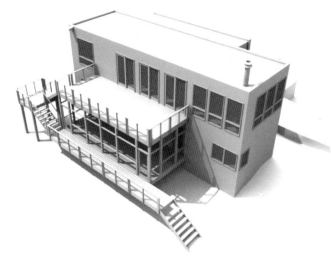

3-D rendering

West elevation

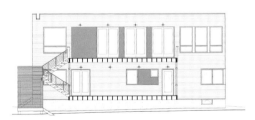

South elevation

Prefabricated construction to reduce CO_2 emissions from transportation and minimize impact on the environment; recycled and recyclable material, such as wood

Photovoltaic panels; geothermal energy

Use of native, drought-resistant plant varieties

The main volume is clad in
cedarwood. Natural materials
with minimum treatment, such as
wood, are the easiest to recycle
or reuse.

East elevation

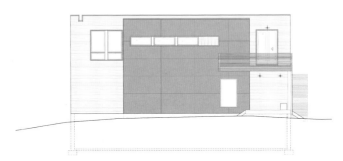

North elevation

This orientation offers the house
the maximum hours of daylight.
Openings are larger on the south
facade, where there is also a large
deck and glass-encased porch.

There are entrances to the house
on both levels. The lower level, with
a study and two guest bedrooms,
has its own entrance. The upper
level is reached via the deck.

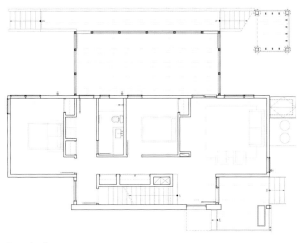

Lower level

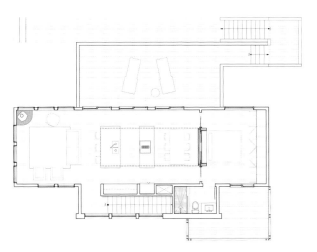

Upper level

To make the most of the views of the surrounding area, the communal areas, the master bedroom, and the terrace are on the upper level, where there is more sunlight during the day.

The kitchen is at the heart of
the upper level and separates
the living area from the dining
area and the bedroom. The
electricity used comes exclusively
from photovoltaic panels and
geothermal energy.

The Eyelid House

Fiona Winzar Architects

Victoria, Australia

190 m² / 2,045 sq. ft.

© Emma Cross

The brief for the architectural firm was to turn a typical Victorian terrace into a contemporary, functional residence for a family of five. The challenge for the architects was to transform the dark and cramped dwelling, located on a narrow plot of land, into a comfortable, light-filled home. Despite the difficulties involved in working on this site, a three-bedroom house was erected.

One of the most striking aspects of the property is a large roof extension imitating the shape of a huge eyelid. This allows a view of the patio while protecting the privacy of the occupants inside the house. This extraordinary shape screens the back of the building from prying neighbors and allows natural light to flood in.

The materials used to construct the new building were chosen to maximize sustainability and protect the environment. For example, the timber used in the structure comes from renewable forests and the paintwork does not contain any toxic substances.

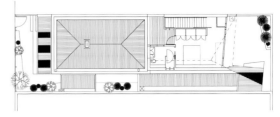

Upper floor

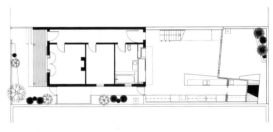

Lower floor

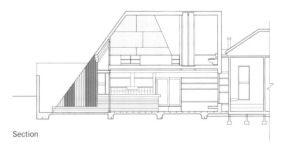

Section

Rainwater collection; water-conserving fixtures

Timber from renewable forests; nontoxic paints

Solar panels

House orientation and large windows to make maximum use of heat and light from the sun and to provide cross ventilation

The use of stained glass and an
arabesque design creates an
exotic atmosphere both inside and
outside the house.

The steps taken to enhance
sustainability and that show
respect for the environment are
the use of renewable materials
and solar panels, plus low energy
consumption and rainwater
collection.

Casa Pulmo

Cathi House/House + House Architects

Cabo Pulmo, Mexico

195 m² / 2,100 sq. ft.

© Steven & Cathi House

Located in the fishing village of Cabo Pulmo, in the south of the Baja California peninsula, this residence was remodeled to extend it and improve its orientation. This action also permitted its foundation to be strengthened and features to be added to turn it into an ecologically sound house. The temperatures in this region are extreme, with strong winter winds and hurricanes. With this climate in mind, the architects of Casa Pulmo made the best use of daylight, cross ventilation, and shade in order to do away with the need for mechanical air-conditioning. Hand built by local workers using local materials, this house offers complete access to wheelchair users, with an entrance ramp bordered by native vegetation. Solar panels on the roof supply the necessary electricity. The thermal mass of the concrete floor slab heats the house in winter and the *palapa* structure, with its thatched roof, provides shade in summer. Rainwater is collected for watering and is treated for domestic use. A central skylight creates a convection current that cools the interior.

Lower level

Upper level

 Rainwater collection for watering; water tanks

 Locally sourced material; built with traditional craft techniques

 Photovoltaic panels

 House orientation to make maximum use of heat and light from the sun and shade and to provide cross ventilation; thermal mass; central skylight to create a convection current to cool the interior

The upper floor contains the
living area, kitchen, and master
bedroom to take advantage of the
magnificent views of the landscape
around the house. Movable glass
walls allow the interior of the house
to be merged with the terraces.

A ramp offers access to the upper
level for wheelchair users. The
path is decorated in earth tones
and with local agave plants.

Elevation

The house was completely
hand built by local craftsmen.
Having been sourced locally,
the materials also contribute to
the environmental balance.

The upper level, practically an
open plan, contains the master
bedroom and bathroom. Views
can be enjoyed from almost
any part of the house.

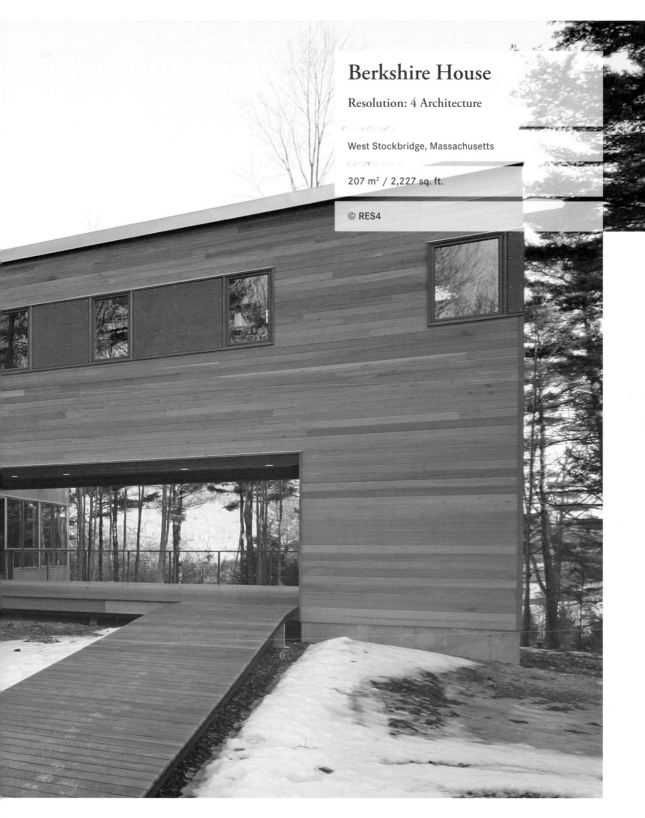

Berkshire House

Resolution: 4 Architecture

West Stockbridge, Massachusetts

207 m² / 2,227 sq. ft.

© RES4

Prefabricated homes are a type of architecture that contributes to environmental sustainability. Prefabricated parts are mostly assembled in factories, reducing environmental impact on the site where only the final installation is carried out. However, even when some parts need to be assembled on-site, less time in construction translates to important cost and energy savings when compared to conventional construction techniques that can last months, even years.

In this case, the house was transported to the site, where the modules making it up were assembled. Featured materials are cedar cladding, bamboo floors, and insulated glass windows and walls.

Geothermal energy is a natural resource that is used for heating and cooling the house. Windows in practically all of the rooms provide natural light and reduce lighting costs. A porch on the lower floor creates open and shaded spaces for the warmest months.

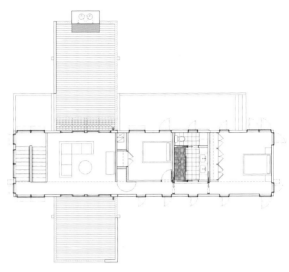

Upper level

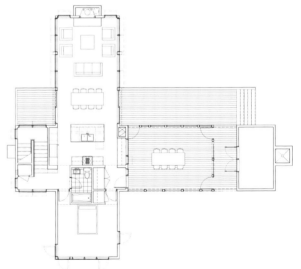

Lower level

Natural and recyclable materials such as bamboo; insulated glass windows and walls

Geothermal energy for heating and cooling; biomass

Prefabricated construction to reduce CO_2 emissions from transportation and minimize impact on the environment

The glass expanses and two upper floor decks blur the boundaries between interior and exterior and offer the occupants the chance to be in greater contact with nature.

The modules were built in a factory, although final assembly was carried out on-site. Fewer workers needing to travel and the shorter construction time reduced CO_2 emissions.

Model

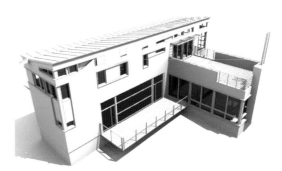

3-D renderings

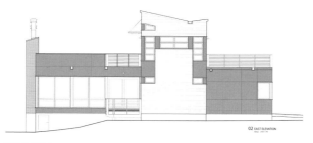

East elevation

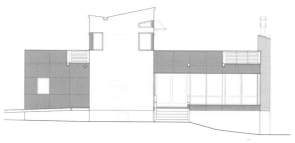

West elevation

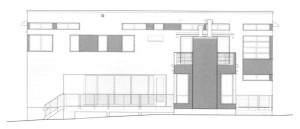

North elevation

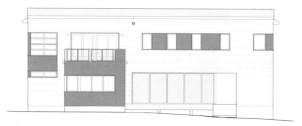

The fireplace on the deck can be used on spring and fall nights. The use of biomass and geothermal energy reduces the use of fossil fuels.

South elevation

The predominant finishes used in
the interior are bamboo flooring,
CaesarStone countertops, slate
bathroom flooring, cherry cabinets,
aluminium-clad wood windows,
insulated glass, and hot-rolled
black steel cladding.

Santa Monica PreFab

Office of Mobile Design by Jennifer Siegal

Santa Monica, California

216 m² / 2,330 sq. ft.

© Laura Hull

This prefabricated home is located on a small lot in the Ocean Park neighborhood. Two of the facades are exposed, while the rest are more enclosed and private. The lower floor contains the garage, kitchen, and living area, while the upper floor contains the bedrooms and an office space. The construction process was carried out in a factory and only the final assembly was on-site, reducing costs and CO_2 emissions. Additionally, most of the materials used follow sustainability criteria. The paints are free of volatile organic compounds (VOCs) and the adhesives are nontoxic. Significant use was made of recycled materials, such as aluminum in the exterior doors and windows, and of insulating materials such as low-emissivity glass, which keeps the heat inside in winter and prevents heat from entering in summer. The floors are bamboo, a natural and recyclable material. Finally, a Takagi water heater only uses energy on demand.

Front and rear elevations

Recycled materials such as aluminum and bamboo; VOC-free paint; nontoxic adhesives; low-maintenance materials such as fiber cement panels

Low-emissivity glass for insulating

Prefabricated construction to reduce CO_2 emissions from transportation and minimize impact on the environment

The Hardiplank fiber-cement panels
require little maintenance and
are more durable than wood and
stucco. They are also fire resistant.

Upper level

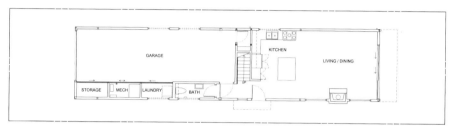

Lower level

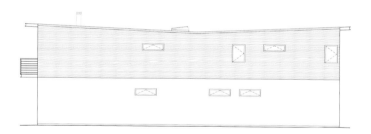

Side elevations

The glass is low-emissivity, which
prevents infrared radiation from
passing through and heating the
interior in summer. It prevents heat
loss from the interior in winter.

Emigration Canyon

Sparano + Mooney Architecture

Emigration Canyon, Utah

232 m² / 2,500 sq. ft.

© Sparano + Mooney Architecture

This single-family residence is located in the vicinity of Salt Lake City. It was designed to capture the views of the canyon and to offer the family a series of communal spaces. The living room has a sliding glass wall that transforms the space into an outdoor room. The design incorporates a number of sustainability criteria; in fact, it was recognized with the first LEED Silver certification in Utah.

Water use is controlled by dual-flush toilets and rainwater collection for outdoor watering. Maximum use is made of natural lighting, with windows and Solatube® skylights letting daylight into the interior. In order to best adapt the building to the climate, weather conditions in the area throughout the year were studied, as were the strict building codes that would define the volume and location of the home. The resulting design captures breezes to cool the house in the summer months. The featured materials—weathered steel, timber, and glass—require little maintenance.

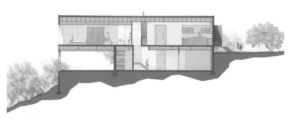

Longitudinal section

Model

Rainwater collection for watering; dual-flush toilets

House orientation to provide cross ventilation; Solatube® skylights and windows to provide natural light

Minimal environmental impact due to design of house; landscaping with native plant species

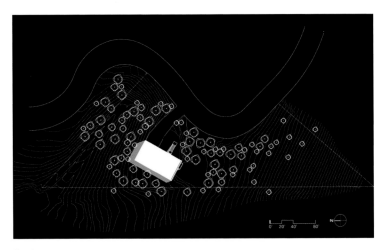

Site plan

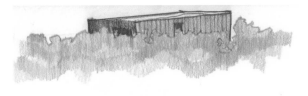

Rendering

Sketch

Building regulations prevented building on more than 30 percent of the hillside. The design did away with the need for excessive excavation and preserved most of the oak trees on the site, resulting in a minimal environmental impact.

The weathered steel cladding is very durable and needs almost no maintenance, reducing the cost of materials. The color of the cladding makes the house blend into its surroundings.

Cross section

The steps leading to the house
were also made from weathered
steel. The durability of this material
makes it ideal for exterior use.

The sloping site required
entrances to the house on
different levels. An original
entrance in the south facade
leads directly to the upper level.

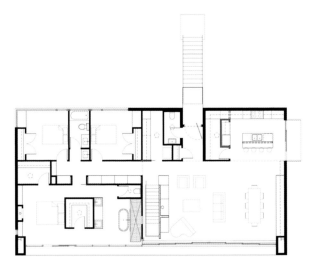

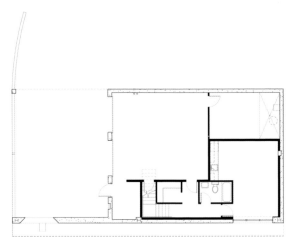

Upper and lower levels

Wood interiors create warm
and comfortable spaces. Glass
expanses provide exclusively
natural lighting during the day.

Residence O

Andrea Tognon Architecture

Teolo, Italy

250 m² / 2,690 sq. ft.

© Andrea Tognon

The original house was built in the 1970s in the style of the vernacular architecture of the Veneto region, although the result was not very satisfactory. This project turned an L-shaped floor plan into a full square. Another important action was taken on the roof of the house. The old roof, inelegant and disproportionate, was modified to redefine the joints of the outer walls. The interior layout was totally changed. All of the walls and ceilings were insulated with Styrodur® panels. This material reduces CO_2 emissions, as the foam cells contain nothing other than air, containing only extruded polystyrene foam (XPS) that is free of CFCs, HCFCs, and HFCs. The house's thermal insulation was also significantly improved. Radiant heating was installed, fed by solar panels. Window glass and frames were replaced with insulated versions.

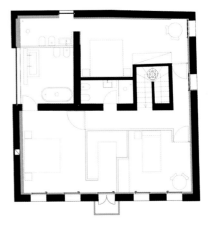

Upper level

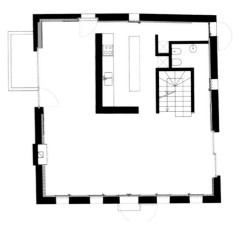

Lower level

Styrodur® insulation panels; insulated windows and frames

Solar thermal panels for heating

The interior layout was changed
completely. New wall and
ceiling panels increase the
thermal insulation of the house,
reducing the need for heating,
which is from solar power.

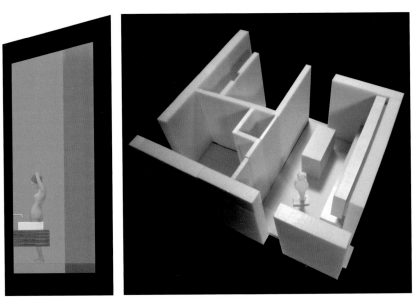

Model

3-D renderings

The remodeling of the residence improved both its appearance and the sustainable aspects of its architecture. Large insulated expanses of glass let in more daylight while retaining heat inside.

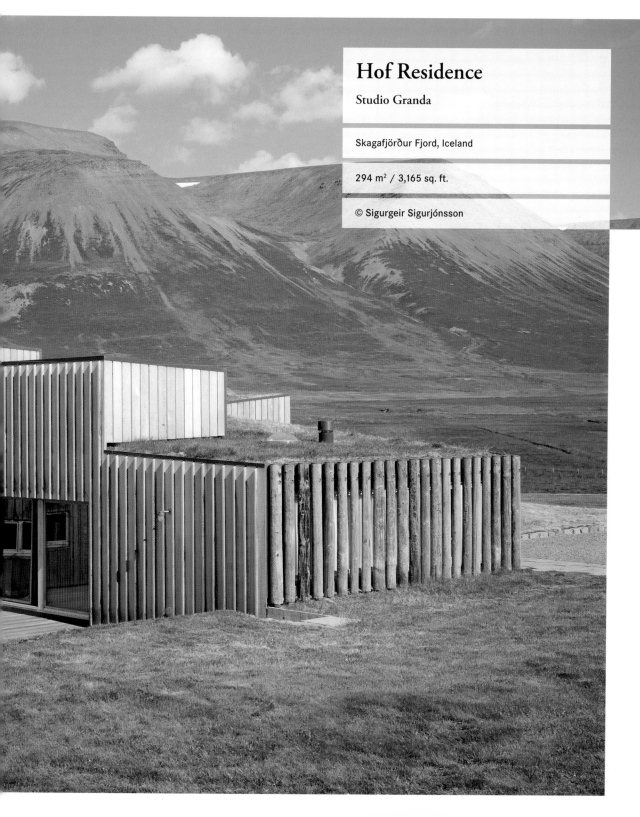

Hof Residence

Studio Granda

Skagafjörður Fjord, Iceland

294 m² / 3,165 sq. ft.

© Sigurgeir Sigurjónsson

The Hof Residence is set in the midst of imposing and spectacular scenery: Skagafjörður Fjord, less than 66 miles (106 km) from the Arctic Circle. The old estate buildings are still present in this remote setting, near a valley that is well known for breeding horses. The excellent rapport built up between clients, builder, and architects led to a new site being chosen and a distinct design, in which every space in the house is oriented to capture the magnificent panorama.

The outer walls are concrete with cedar cladding, which will wear with the passing of time. Some of the roof areas have been planted with grass to improve insulation and help maintain a steady temperature in the house. Along with the large windows, which allow natural light to flood the house, a number of skylights were installed in the roof to light different rooms. The house is well insulated by solid concrete walls and stone floors. Heating and hot water are provided through geothermal energy, a common resource in volcanic countries such as Iceland. Electricity use has been reduced as the required power is supplied from hydroelectric and geothermal sources.

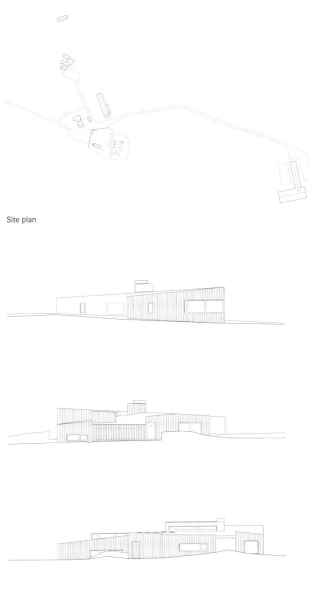

Site plan

Elevations

 Locally sourced and natural materials; reused materials

 Geothermal and hydroelectric energy

Large windows, skylights, and well-positioned rooms to provide natural light; thermal mass; green roof; concrete walls and stone floors to act as insulation

The old house with stables, a church, and a barn are located near the new site. New stables were built farther inland.

The grass that covers the property
was also planted on the roofs,
helping to insulate the house.
Skylights, which allow light into
the rooms, are also evident.

Floor plan

The dark basalt rock, dug out
when the foundation was laid,
was reused in exterior areas
and in communal and transit
spaces inside the house.

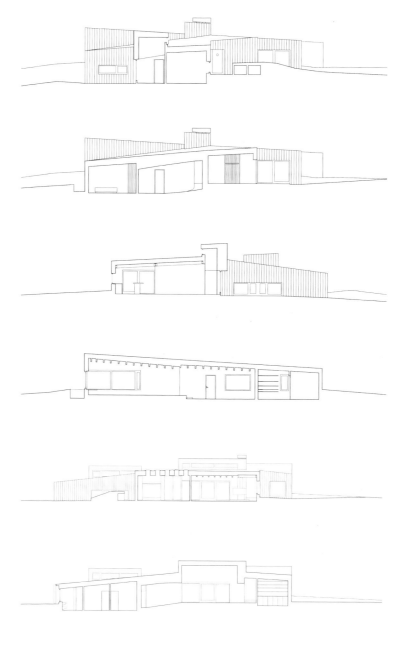

The layout of the spaces features rooms oriented to enjoy the views and capture natural light. A unique structure was created, with blocks that look separate from the outside.

Sections

Directory

@6 Architecture
San Francisco, CA
www.at-six.com

Andersson Wise Architects
Austin, TX
www.anderssonwise.com

Andrea Tognon Architecture
Milan, Italy
www.atognon.com

Arconiko Architecten
Rotterdam, The Netherlands
www.arconiko.com

Arkhefield
Brisbane, Australia
www.arkhefield.com.au

BAK Arquitectos
Buenos Aires, Argentina
www.bakarquitectos.com.ar

Bercy Chen Studio
Austin, TX
www.bcarc.com

Bricault Design
Vancouver, Canada
www.bricault.ca

CCS Architecture
San Francisco, CA
www.ccs-architecture.com

Change Architects
Amsterdam, The Netherlands
www.changearchitects.nl

Correia/Ragazzi Arquitectos
Oporto, Portugal
www.correiaragazzi.com

Craig Steely Architecture
San Francisco, CA
craigsteely.com

Ecosistema Urbano Arquitectos
Madrid, Spain
www.ecosistemaurbano.com

Fantastic Norway Architects
Oslo, Norway
www.fantasticnorway.no

Fiona Winzar Architects
Melbourne, Australia
www.fionawinzar.com

FLOAT Architectural Research and Design
Portland, OR
www.floatwork.com

H Arquitectes
Sabadell, Spain
www.harquitectes.com

Hampson Williams
London, United Kingdom
www.hampsonwilliams.com

Hangar Design Group
Mogliano Veneto, Italy
www.hangar.it

House + House Architects
San Francisco, CA
www.houseandhouse.com

Jeffrey McKean Architect
New York, NY
www.jeffreymckean.com

Marc Koehler Architects
Amsterdam, The Netherlands
www.marckoehler.nl

Marmol Radziner Prefab
Los Angeles, CA
www.marmolradzinerprefab.com

Max Pritchard Architect
Adelaide, Australia
www.maxpritchardarchitect.com.au

Morphosis Architects
Santa Monica, CA
www.morphosis.com

Obie G. Bowman
Healdsburg, CA
www.obiebowman.com

Office of Mobile Design by Jennifer Siegal
Venice, CA
www.designmobile.com

OFIS Arhitekti
Ljubljana, Slovenia
www.ofis-a.si

Petr Hájek Architekti
Prague, Czech Republic
www.hajekarchitekti.cz

Resolution: 4 Architecture
New York, NY
re4a.com

Shaun Lockyer Architects
Brisbane, Australia
www.lockyerarchitects.com.au

Sparano + Mooney Architecture
Los Angeles, CA
www.sparanomooney.com

Studio 804
Laurence, KS
www.studio804.com

Studio Granda
Reykjavik, Iceland
www.studiogranda.is

Taalman Koch Architecture
Los Angeles, CA
www.tkarchitecture.com

Turnbull Griffin Haesloop
San Francisco, CA
www.tgharchitects.com

UCArchitect
Toronto, Canada
www.ucarchitect.ca

University of Illinois
Urbana, IL
www.illinois.edu